Agile Principles, Values, and Best Practices

Agile Practitioners' Perspectives and Insights Series

First Edition

The *Pass Certification Assessments at the First Attempt* Series

This **new** series replaces the previous *Pass Certification Assessments at the First Attempt* series. Since the publication of *Scrum Fundamentals*, there have been significant changes introduced by **Scrum Alliance** as well as **Scrum.org**. The Scrum certification paths have changed considerably, with the addition of multiple types and levels of certification. Accordingly, the scope and content of the training programs and assessments have also undergone a complete overhaul. This series aims to demystify the increasingly complex world of certifications and their usefulness.

Each book in this series seeks to act as a *single* and *comprehensive* source of *focused* information on **how to pass select Certification assessments.** This information includes relevant details on the certification and the assessment; a strategy to prepare for and take the assessment; and finally, adequate study material for the assessment itself. None of these books is aimed at providing *comprehensive* details on Scrum theory or practices. The other book series, *Agile Practitioners' Perspectives and Insights*, does just that. Please evaluate the various book options to find ones that meet your needs.

The first book is targeted at those who are interested in getting a better understanding of *Agile and Scrum Certification* – the credentials and assessments. They may wish to explore further, on their own, the available educational and training resources to pass these assessments.

The second book is for those who may have a *basic* or *intermediate* experience in, or knowledge of, Scrum. It provides a complete *overview* required for passing Level I Scrum assessments. It also includes additional background information, which may not be required for these assessments.

The third and fourth books are for those who already have a *basic* or *intermediate* experience in, or knowledge of, Scrum. These books provide *focused* study material targeted at helping those who wish to obtain Level I and II **Scrum Master** credentials.

The fifth and sixth books are for those who already have a *basic* or *intermediate* experience in, or knowledge of, Scrum. These books provide *focused* study material targeted at helping those who wish to obtain Level I and II **Product Owner** credentials.

The seventh book is for those who may have an *advanced* experience in, or knowledge of, Scrum. It provides very *focused* study material required to obtain Level III **Scrum Master and/or Product Owner** credentials.

Note: Aspirants may, based on their background and the assessment they wish to take, opt for *only one* amongst the five *Fundamentals* or *Foundational and Intermediate* Scrum guides listed below. The only exceptions to this 'rule' are the *first* and *last* books, each of which has its own unique content.

If you are interested in both the *Scrum Master* and *Product Owner* credentials, you may opt for one book for *Scrum Master* assessments and another one for *Product Owner* assessments. Though there is significant degree of overlap in content, common between the two, each book has its own focus areas based on the role.

Vol.	Title	Expected Launch Date
1.	Agile and Scrum Certification: A Comprehensive Overview	Q1-2021
2.	Scrum Fundamentals: A Complete Guide for Level I Certification Assessments	Q1-2021
3.	Foundational and Intermediate Scrum for CSM and A-CSM Certification	Q1-2021
4.	Foundational and Intermediate Scrum for PSM I and PSM II Certification	Q1-2021
5.	Foundational and Intermediate Scrum for CSPO and A-CSPO Certification	Q2-2021
6.	Foundational and Intermediate Scrum for PSPO I and PSPO II Certification	Q2-2021
7.	Advanced Scrum for Level III Scrum Master and Product Owner Certification	Q3-2021

For more information, please send an email to: xyepress@xyberg.com

The *Agile Practitioners' Perspectives and Insights* Series

This series provides *perspectives and insights*, primarily in the form of practical *field guides*, for various stakeholders. Each book in this series seeks to act as a *fairly comprehensive* source of information as well as to provide *unique* perspectives on a specific *focus area*.

The first book is targeted at those interested in getting a deeper understanding of *Agile Principles* and how they relate to *Agile Best Practices*. This book provides the 'missing link' between the *Principles* and *Practices*, in order to effectively respond to the oft-asked question – *why are we not completely Agile yet?* Most folks pay cursory attention to the principles and dive right into 'practicing' Agile. This often results in development of anti-patterns and *'non-Agile'* behavior or attitude, which in turn results in a *'non-Agile'* team or organizational mindset and culture.

The second book serves as a ***practical field guide***, which helps team members to quickly ramp up their understanding of Agile processes and best practices. It describes the processes and practices applicable to every step in the journey. This will help team members to not only set up right expectations but also apply contextual knowledge and skills effectively, for every significant action required on a daily basis.

The third book, targeted at team members and leadership of Agile teams as well as peripheral teams, describes various approaches to set up and launch new Agile teams. It also takes readers through the various phases of development and maturity that these teams go through: how teams form, storm and norm and ultimately perform. It provides an alternative perspective to the previous book – the field guide – but it also guides team members on each step of the team's evolution, from a practical perspective.

The fourth book compares and contrasts the two approaches: Scrum and Kanban. It provides contextual information on *when* either of these is more relevant. It also guides leadership and team members how and why *Kanban* or *Scrum* teams are set up and deployed. It describes best practices and how they complement each other; and why a *Scrumban* model can be more appropriate in certain cases.

The fifth book enables organizations and teams to navigate the Agile adoption and transformation journey, particularly during the transition from traditional or Waterfall model and methodologies. It describes various phases of evolution and end-states; and practical steps to be taken in each phase. The book also considers various challenges along the way and how to navigate or address them.

The sixth book focuses on various factors, which determine how an organization's culture evolves and how effective interventions result in desired outcomes. This book helps to analyze the *human* component of organization and Agile teams: Group Dynamics (GD), Organizational Behavior (OB) and Organizational Development (OD). It addresses the *attitudinal, behavioral and personality* aspects from the individual, team and organizational perspectives.

The seventh book is targeted at Leaders for developing effective *Agile vision, strategies and implementation plan*s. It is helpful for organizations, which are either starting their Agile Journey or launching new Scrum Teams, or already at different levels of maturity in the Agile journey. Leaders could use either a top-down, or bottom-up approach, or a mix of the two, to develop a truly Agile organization. It also focuses on how teams achieve stability at the earliest and continually enhance their performance levels.

The eight book addresses the *Scaling needs*, at a *limited scale*, as a natural extension or progression in the Agile journey. It is relevant for startups, and small- or mid-sized organizations, which need to scale to few teams for a product or a department. For instance, if there are about 10 teams working in concert on a product, where a model like Nexus may be more relevant.

The ninth book addresses the *Scaling Conundrum for large organizations and enterprises – design for scale* at the beginning; or later, when large-scale scaling needs arise. It recommends the development of a *custom* Enterprise scaled model, which would best meet the organization's needs, based on the best elements of the Large-Scale Scrum (LeSS), Scaled Agile Framework (SAFe), Spotify and other models.

Vol.	Title	Expected Launch Date
1.	Agile Principles, Values, and Best Practices	Q1-2021
2.	Scrum Field Guide for Agile Teams	Q2-2021
3.	Launching Scrum Teams: Form, Storm, Norm and Perform	Q2-2021
4.	Scrum and Kanban Best Practices	Q2-2021
5.	Agile Adoption and Transformation: Waterfall to Agile Transition	Q3-2021
6.	Agile Cultural Transformation	Q3-2021
7.	Agile for Leaders: Successful Agile Vision, Strategy and Execution	Q4-2021
8.	Agile Adoption and Transformation: Scaling and Performing	Q4-2021
9.	Agile Adoption and Transformation: Enterprise Scaled Agile Models	Q4-2021

For more information, please send an email to: xyepress@xyberg.com

Agile Principles, Values, and Best Practices

Agile Practitioners' Perspectives and Insights Series

First Edition

Feroz Khan

CSM, PSM I, PMP

Acknowledgements:

The author wishes to acknowledge and thank the owners of copyrights of the material, as well as the source of *royalty free* stock images, used in this book.

Cover Page Photo: Victor He, *Garden by the Bay, Singapore*

Website: www.unsplash.com

Table of Contents

List of Tables and Figures

About the Author

Over a career spanning 20+ years, Feroz Khan has held various delivery leadership roles in the Software and Information Technology industry in the US. He has led large teams, at companies like Tech Mahindra and Zensar Technologies, India's 5th and 20th largest Software Services companies, respectively, serving few Fortune 100 clients.

His passion for software development started in high school in 1983, when the industry was still in a nascent stage. After a few initial years as an IT Market Analyst, software developer, systems analyst and project manager, he led product development initiatives as a Marketing Manager and Product Manager. Later, he decided to focus on the *delivery* aspect of software programs and projects. Over the last fifteen years or so, he became progressively involved in solution architecture, project, program and portfolio management and held senior leadership positions.

Since 2000, Feroz has successfully led several hundreds of projects – large and small – developing *enterprise solutions* for startups, SMEs and Fortune 500 companies. These include market leaders like Cisco Systems, Apple, Equinix, Santen Pharmaceuticals, Bank of the West, Wells Fargo and Project Management Institute (PMI). He has been actively involved in championing and implementing Agile and Hybrid methodologies since 2006. In the last ten years or so, he has led or actively participated in a few Agile adoption and transformation initiatives. During the same period, he has championed adoption of Cloud and Interconnection strategies; and led development of eCommerce, Digital, and XaaS platforms or solutions.

In 2010, Feroz Khan founded *Xyberg Systems* (pronounced as *Cybergie Systems*) to provide *Software Development* and *IT Consulting* services to Fortune 500 companies, particularly in the areas of methodologies, process design, and program or project execution.

Preface

In the real world, Agile practices may differ significantly from what many Agile experts prescribe. I have intentionally used the word 'prescribe', because that's what many Agile experts do. Agile frameworks, models and methodologies are *not* supposed to be prescriptive at all. However, experts and coaches tend to exhort teams and individuals to practice Agile methodologies and techniques in a 'pure' or 'ideal' way. As a result of this, I have often been asked what's the right way to do something. I almost always answer: 'it depends'. More often than not, there's never a 'right' way. In the 'Agile world', there is nothing that is absolutely right or wrong. There is only a *suitable* way...the 'best' way or the 'normal' way, which depends on the individual's or team's own situation and context. This is where *Norms* and *Best Practices* come in. Teams may develop their own norms under a broader organizational framework or standards. Organizations should find the right balance between standardization or consistency, and flexibility.

Generally, best practices are 'portable' and can be widely adopted across teams or organizations. However, sometimes, what is good for the goose may *not* always be good for the gander. That is why organizations are encouraged to develop their own Agile models, based on common frameworks and generally accepted best practices.

Two key points must be addressed while developing custom models and best practices. Firstly, there are *just a few rules*, which models must comply with, in order to be considered Agile. For instance, Sprints or iterations must be time-boxed. Teams and organizations should not compromise on the basic rules. Nonetheless, the number of such rules should be minimized. Secondly, practices should not devolve into *anti-patterns*. In the end, we are interested in developing software that delights customers. Processes and practices are just the *means* to achieve that end. These should entail minimum overheads.

Each book in this series highlights some critical aspect of Agile frameworks, model, methodologies, techniques, processes and practices. Readers may use the insights presented in these books, to develop a better understanding of Agile models and best practices.

-- Feroz Khan

Part 1: Introduction

This Part provides the **Purpose of this book,** its **Organization** and a **brief history of Agile and Scrum frameworks**.

A significantly large number of organizations rush into implementing AgileX[1], without being truly ready. Teams are rapidly deployed without adequate training; and are then expected to immediately start delivering working software using the new models. There seems to be a norm in most organizations to conduct a workshop, typically over 2 or 3 days, before launching an Agile team. This training is considered sufficient to start implementing the organization's Agile model. This assumption may not necessarily be correct. These workshops or training programs tend to focus on foundational knowledge and concepts – primarily, the 'structural' aspects of AgileX. Team members, who have attended some kind of training or coaching sessions, would agree that the subject of 'Agile Principles and Values' has not been given due attention or coverage. Most training or coaching programs tend to gloss over this topic.

As a result, teams tend to 'do Agile' rather than 'be Agile'. There is an enormous difference in *Being Agile* and *Doing Agile*. An incorrect or incomplete understanding of the **_Agile Principles and Values_** leads to the *development of anti-patterns*; and, over the long run, a *culture antithetical to Agile principle*s. This book aims to make teams aware of means to address this gap by providing 'the missing link' between Agile best practices and the underlying principles.

---

[1] X represents Frameworks, Models, Methodologies, Processes, Practices and the like

Chapter 1: Purpose of this Book and the Book Series

The only purpose of this book is to help readers gain a **better understanding of Agile Principles and Values:** to help them *understand and implement Agile models better, by adopting best practices and avoiding anti-patterns*. It does *not* provide 'complete' details on *Agile* frameworks, models, methodologies, processes, principles and practices.

The *'Agile Practitioners' Perspectives and Insights'* book series has been developed primarily from my own experience. It is based on learning, acquired from various experts along the way, on a continuous basis, what it takes to *'Being Agile'* rather than just *'Doing Agile'*. A continual endeavor shall be made to enhance the coverage and effectiveness of the content in these books.

Chapter 2: Organization of this Book

Part 1 of this book provides an **introduction**: the **purpose** of this book and how it is **organized**; as well as a **brief history** of how _Agile frameworks_ generally developed. Throughout this book, there is a significant focus on _Scrum_ because it is the most popular amongst all Agile frameworks and models. In addition, _Scrum_ constitutes the basic building block, which lies at the core of most scaled frameworks and models. This book does _not_ intend to provide a deep exposure to various Agile frameworks, models and methodologies. The focus is on _Agile Principles and Values_, with some exposure to _Best Practices_ based on these principles and values.

Part 2 provides an overview of the **Agile Principles and Values**, as well as a _**brief introduction to Agile Software Development**_, based on principles and practices common across various models and methodologies.

In each chapter of **Part 3**, each **Agile Principle** is described and assessed in more detail. Few _**best practices**_ are presented to provide a better understanding on how these relate to one or more of the underlying principles. This will hopefully result in a better appreciation of the principles and values, which will help in the development of best practices and an Agile mindset. A continual attempt will be made, over the next few years, to provide more insights and contextual information.

Chapter 3: A Brief History of Agile Frameworks

Anyone who has been involved with software development, in some capacity or role, will be aware that organizations have adopted _AgileX_ very rapidly in the past few years. After experimenting with these methodologies and models over a decade ago, early adopters have achieved huge successes in transforming their delivery models. Some have been quite successful in transforming their organization culture. Yet, today, most organizations continue to have a mix of the traditional Waterfall and the 'new' Agile models. Some experts believe that the hybrid model is here to stay and a 'pure Agile' model will always be out of reach. Nonetheless, these continuous efforts to migrate to Agile models provide individuals with greater opportunities to learn and become a part of this journey.

Contrary to what most believe, Agile methodologies and models are not really 'new'. The word 'Agile', in the context of software development, is considered to have been 'coined' in 2001 during the OOPSLA[2] conference at the Snowbird ski resort in Utah.

Seventeen experts and thought-leaders of the software development community got together, formed the **_Agile Alliance_**, and developed the **_Manifesto for Agile Software Development_** aka the **_Agile Manifesto_**. The term 'Agile' came to represent few models and methodologies, such as _Scrum, Extreme Programming (XP), Adaptive Software Development (ASD), Dynamic Systems Development Method (DSDM), Feature-Driven Development (FDD), Crystal, Pragmatic Programming_, and so on, which have been in existence since the early 1990s.

Martin Fowler, one of the founders of the _Agile Alliance_, has provided a brief, yet excellent, recap on the origins of the _Alliance_ and few interesting developments at the OOPSLA conference: https://martinfowler.com/articles/agileStory.html. Robert Martin, popularly known as _Uncle Bob_, also has presented some recollections and thoughts at: https://sites.google.com/site/unclebobconsultingllc/the-founding-of-the-agile-alliance.

---

[2] OOPSLA (Object-Oriented Programming, Systems, Languages & Applications) is an annual ACM research conference. Association for Computing Machinery (ACM) is a US-based non-profit professional membership organization.

Figure 1.1: Agile: An Umbrella Term

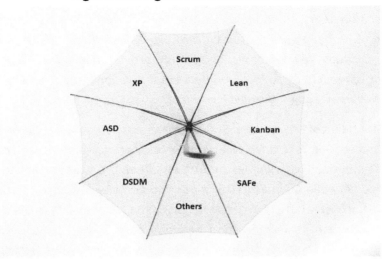

There has been some debate on the nomenclature of the Manifesto, with a number of practitioners and experts objecting to the usage of the term *'Agile Manifesto'*. They believe that the word 'Agile' should qualify *Software Development* rather than the *Manifesto,* as originally conceived in *'Manifesto for Agile Software Development'*. Few have, semi-seriously, observed that the Manifesto itself is 'not so Agile'. Nonetheless, the Manifesto has proven to be a sound basis for a revolution that has touched, if not transformed, all industries in recent years. More details on its history, which is a very interesting reading, can be found at: https://agilemanifesto.org/history.html

There has also been a debate about whether the word 'Agile' is an adjective or a noun. Without getting too much into semantics, the author wishes to call out that a lexicon develops out of usage in a colloquial sense, rather than just through a formal prescription or recommendation, as in a dictionary or thesaurus. In this book, the term has been loosely used, in reference to the context.

Scrum, as you probably already know, is currently the most popular of all Agile frameworks, models and methodologies. The word 'Scrum', derived from 'scrummage' in the game of rugby, was first used by *Hirotaka Takeuchi* and *Ikujiro Nonaka*, in the context of product development. Their HBR article[3] highlighted a new *product development approach*, to be followed by a *cross-functional team*, which *continuously delivers innovation* through *iterative increments*.

The two co-founders of Scrum – *Ken Schwaber* and *Jeff Sutherland* – were influenced by this paper and applied it to develop an **empirical**, **iterative** and **incremental** *software development approach* for **complex adaptive systems**[4]. It is important to understand the difference between *Complicated Systems* and *Complex Systems*. To state it simply, in a Complicated System, there are many, many parts but they interact with each other in a very *specific* way. The interaction between parts is well understood and fairly consistent, except at the time when the parts break down. By understanding each of the parts and their interactions, it is possible to understand the system as a whole. In other words, the system is a sum of its parts, however complicated. On the other hand, in a complex system, the parts may interact with each other, through a feedback loop, in an *evolving* and *adaptive* manner. The system is <u>not</u> just a sum of its parts. Due to its evolving and adaptive nature, we can only analyze and understand snapshots; but never the system, in its entirety, at any or all times.

In the early 1990s, Ken developed the approach at his company, Advanced Development Methods, working with *Mike Smith* and *Chris Martin*. Similarly, Jeff Sutherland created the Scrum methodology, along with *Jeff McKenna* and *John Scumniotales*, and started the very first Scrum team at Easel Corporation in 1993. Later, Ken Schwaber and Jeff Sutherland worked together to integrate their approaches and develop the Scrum framework. They jointly presented a paper on the framework at the OOPSLA conference at Austin, Texas, in 1995; and formalized the Scrum framework. This paper introduced a revolutionary way of developing software; and perhaps was not very well appreciated then, considering that Scrum became widely popular only in the early 2000's.

---

[3] See their article, *'The New New Product Development Game'* published in Harvard Business Review in 1986

[4] Kevin Dooley defined Complex Adaptive System (CAS) as a group of semi-autonomous agents who interact in interdependent ways to produce system-wide patterns, such that those patterns then influence behavior of the agents. Source: Human Systems Dynamics Institute

This paper, *must read* for any Agile practitioner, is still available at:

http://www.jeffsutherland.org/oopsla/schwapub.pdf,

and at:

https://scrumorg-website-prod.s3.amazonaws.com/drupal/2016-09/Scrum%20OOPSLA%201995.pdf.

Ken and Jeff co-authored **The Scrum Guide[5],** the first version of which was published in 2010; and the latest in 2020. Since 2010, there have been several iterations and various contributors. **The Scrum Guide is considered 'the Bible of Scrum'** – it is another *must-read*. For a more complete history on the evolution of the Guide, please refer to:

https://medium.com/serious-scrum/the-evolution-of-the-scrum-guide-10-to-19-f3ac4d82cfcb

Scrum is considered a **framework** because, by design, it is not meant to be a 'complete' model, so that it will:

- **Restrict the degree of *prescriptiveness* and keep it *simple*;** The number of 'rules' are limited. Note that if these rules are not diligently followed, the model is NOT considered Scrum; and may be referred to as 'Scrum-but', or 'Scrum-like' but not 'Scrum'.
- **Keep the model *flexible* to allow organizations to adopt different approaches in *specific* areas** such as Requirements management, Architecture, Project Management, Release management, and so on. Scrum does not prescribe the *User Story* approach of *Requirements Management;* yet, it is the most popular approach. Organizations are free to adopt their own approaches to 'fill in the intentional gaps' of Scrum. Quite a few organizations continue to use the *Use Case* methodology or a mix of the two. There are pros and cons for each approach. When practitioners try to force fit the User Story approach in every situation, it not only negates the original intent but also results in some humorous outcomes. Consider the following: *As a Thermometer, I want to measure the room temperature so that someone can read it.* As the term 'User' in User Story indicates, it is very important to understand *who the User is* and

---

[5] The Scrum Guide is available at: https://www.scrumguides.org/. This is the first book that a Scrum practitioner must read.

what the *User's purpose* is. This story may be rewritten as: *As an occupant of a room, I would like to know the temperature of the room so that I can maintain a comfortable ambient temperature*. The thermostat, or the thermometer, is the *solution*.

In other words, Frameworks have 'gaps' that need to be filled in to become a model. These gaps allow organizations to adopt suitable techniques or methodologies, which meet their needs. As opposed to framework, a model must be 'complete' to be practical and executable.

Ken and Jeff, amongst several others, have been responsible for promoting the awareness and adoption of Scrum. They have made significant contributions in establishing organizations, which are involved in developing the Scrum and Agile 'body of knowledge'. In addition, these organizations connect and help practitioners to identify, adopt, and promote Agile best practices and skills. These organizations, such as the *Scrum Alliance*, *Scrum.org*, and *Scrum, Inc.*, offer a wide range of individual and corporate training programs, seminars, workshops, conferences and meet-ups.

Ken was responsible for founding the **Scrum Alliance** and creating the *Certified Scrum Master* program and its derivatives. He left the **Scrum Alliance** in the fall of 2009 and then founded **Scrum.org** to 'improve the quality and effectiveness of Scrum'.

Jeff Sutherland founded **Scrum, Inc.**, which was more focused on training and consulting. Until very recently, *Scrum, Inc* did not provide its own certification program and credentials. It conducted training for *Scrum Alliance* certification. In August 2019, *Scrum, Inc* introduced the *Licensed Scrum Program* and modified it significantly in 2020.

The Scrum framework has worked very well for Agile implementations spanning across a few teams, or for smaller organizations. However, for larger organizations and enterprises, it quickly ran into scaling challenges. *Scaled Scrum* models address these challenges to a large degree. Over the years, two different approaches became quite popular:

- **Large-Scale Scrum (LeSS)**
- **Scaled Agile Framework (SAFe)**

In the last few years, the **Spotify model** has also become very popular. A number of organizations have adopted a mix of SAFe, Spotify and LeSS to develop their own custom models. More details on these models are provided in other books in this series.

Scrum.org and *Scrum, Inc.* have also introduced their scaled frameworks – the **Nexus**™ **Framework** (*Scrum.org*) in 2015, and the **Scrum@Scale** framework (*Scrum, Inc.* in association with *Scrum Alliance*) in 2018.

In order to use a model that most closely meets their needs, several organizations have rapidly developed and deployed their own customized frameworks and models. They have cherry-picked the best practices from various approaches, methodologies and frameworks. As a result, it has become quite important for aspirants to be familiar with, and have experience in, more than one approach or model.

Part 2: Introduction to Agile Principles and Values

This Part provides a brief **introduction to Agile Software Development models, the Agile Manifesto, Agile Values, Agile Principles** and **Scrum Values**.

A high-level overview, of each topic is provided in this part of the book. This will help the reader to see the big picture before diving down into details. This book does not provide details on any framework, model or methodology. Another book in this series will probably provide what you need on these, or related, topics.

Chapter 1: Introduction to Agile Software Development

Due to the immense popularity of **Scrum** and limited exposure to, and experience in, other models or frameworks, people tend to use _Scrum_ and _Agile_ interchangeably. This is not correct. Scrum is Agile, but Agile is not Scrum; Or, just Scrum. There are several Agile models, which constitute a happy mix of frameworks, methodologies, structures, principles, processes, and practices.

Any approach, methodology, framework or model, which is consistent with the **_Agile Values_** listed in the **Agile Manifesto**, and the **Agile Principles,** qualify to be referred to as 'Agile'.

It is very important to understand one aspect of the _Agile Manifesto_ very well. We, as Agilists, should value the items on the _left_ **more** than those on the _right_; however, it does **not** mean that the items on the _right_ have no value at all. For instance, _some_ documentation may be quite important, while _comprehensive_ documentation is not. The notion of _value_ also depends on the _established standards_ and _best practices_ of an organization.

A **_Minimum Viable Bureaucracy_** (**MVB**), i.e., the _simplest_ process and structure, with _minimal_ overheads, is required to sustain an organization's Agile model. MVB promotes a degree of 'standardization' across the enterprise to enhance a _common_ or _shared understanding_ of _processes and practices_ as well as _stakeholder expectations_; while seeking a balance between extremes. It also allows for _flexibility_ and _innovation_ suitable to each _individual_ team.

Figure 2.1: Xyberg's Simple Unified Model

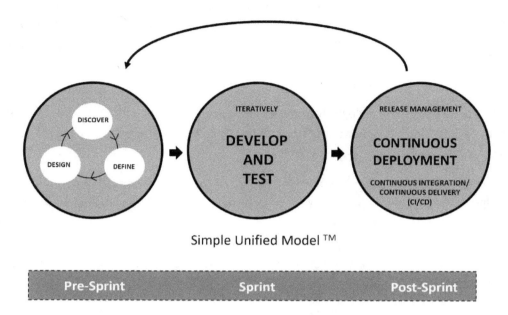

Simple Unified Model ™

Pre-Sprint	Sprint	Post-Sprint

A popular quiz in Agile circles goes: How do you eat an elephant?

The appropriate response?

One bite at a time!

In the 'Agile world', it implies that software should be developed **incrementally** during time-boxed **iterations**. In Scrum, the iterations are *Sprints*; and the increments are the *Product Increments, the 'pieces' of software,* which result after the completion of activities reflected in a *Sprint Backlog* after every Sprint.

Figure 2.1 shows Xyberg's **Simple Unified Model** ™, which is based on various concepts, principles and practices derived from existing Agile models and approaches such as Scrum, SAFe, Design Thinking, Lean Startup, and User Experience Design. Each circle indicates an iterative workflow.

The horizontal bar shows, *as an example*, a *possible* mapping to the Scrum framework.

Pre-Sprint activities may include setting up a framework/model, staffing the Scrum team, procuring and deploying tools and environments, iterative long-term Version/Release planning and management activities, and Backlog management. All of these activities undergo iterative planning, discovery, definition, and design. More detailed insights on these aspects are provided in other books in this series.

The Sprint includes all ***four* formal events** of Scrum, aside from the actual development and testing activities and 'lightweight' release activities at the culmination of the Sprint. The four formal Sprint events are *Sprint Planning, Daily Scrum, Sprint Review* and *Sprint Retrospective*. *Refinement* aka *Backlog Refinement*[6] is a *'non-formal'* activity, running concurrently with the Sprint. The goal of this 'offline' activity is to have, before a Sprint starts, as many READY stories as possible - typically, sufficient for intake into two or three Sprints, in advance.

Post-Sprint activities may include *Release Demos or Retrospectives* or any elaborate Release activities; for instance, if coordination is required between multiple *Release Trains*, or if the team's code is to be deployed in an integrated fashion with that of teams following Waterfall methodologies.

At the heart of the *Scrum Framework* is the **Sprint**, which is a timeboxed iteration. The Sprint duration typically ranges from 1 through 4 weeks. Once a suitable Sprint duration is selected, it is not meant to be changed. Some organizations tend to start with a Sprint duration of 1 week. This encourages rapid experimentation and helps teams to fail fast. However, few organizations may believe that not much is accomplished in a short sprint; and, frequent iterations may result in higher overheads and waste. These organizations tend to opt for longer Sprints, typically 3 or 4 weeks. After experimentation, most organizations seem to have decided that 2 weeks is the optimal duration. This seems to strike a 'happy' balance between delivering software frequently and minimizing overheads.

---

[6] Scrum does not consider *Refinement* as a formal event. This activity should no longer be referred to as 'Grooming'.

The Sprint starts with **Sprint Planning**, during which the Product Owner shares a potential **Sprint Goal** with the team, as a step towards achieving the overall **Product Goal**. The whole team collectively discusses what it takes to accomplish this goal, and then collaboratively finalizes the team's Sprint Goal. The team then agrees to pull a set of *Product Backlog Items (PBIs)* or *stories* from the *Product Backlog* into the Sprint to fulfill the Sprint Goal.

The Development Team then creates a **Sprint Plan** by decomposing the PBIs and identifying Tasks to fulfill the Sprint Goal. This Sprint Plan will eventually be executed and monitored through a Daily Plan. Typically, tasks are associated with individual User Stories, and may be referred to as *Sub-tasks of a User Story*. Sometimes, tasks are generic or span across multiple stories. These become standalone Tasks, which may have their own sub-tasks. As an example, teams may tend to call out 'Coding' and 'Testing', aside from several others, as sub-tasks of a Story. 'Set up test data for Sprint 12' is an example of a standalone Task, which may require some activity *common* to more than one Story in the Sprint. The Sprint Goal, the PBIs, and the Sprint Plan becomes the **Sprint Backlog**.

On each day of the Sprint, during the **Daily Scrum**, the Development team creates a plan for the upcoming work day, i.e., the duration between two consecutive Daily Scrums. The team evaluates the previous day's plan and its accomplishments[7]. Any delays and inhibitors, which may have prevented planned accomplishments, are called out so that these can be addressed post haste, and does not prevent the team's further progress. The upcoming day's plan is then finalized and agreed upon. This includes the planned resolution of any past and current blockers and inhibitors.

Scrum team members are very familiar with the '3 questions' for the Daily Scrum:

- What did you do yesterday?
- What will you do today?
- Are there any impediments in your way?

---

[7] If the first activity on the first day of the Sprint is Sprint Planning, as it should normally be, then the Daily Scrum is not required. Planning for the day is accomplished during Sprint Planning.

I have observed the 'best practice' amongst many teams wherein each team member, in turn, rattles off the answers to these 3 questions during the Daily Scrum. Actually, this is not a very good practice.

In a previous version of the Scrum Guide, these three questions were provided as guidance on what to focus on during the Daily Scrum. A number of 'experts', Scrum Masters and Coaches started propagating the use of these questions during the Daily Scrum. As a result, teams have diligently adopted this 'best practice'. This is not required; and, the Scrum Guide has been updated to reflect that. These three questions are no longer listed in the Scrum Guide, which now states that the purpose of the Daily Scrum is to **inspect progress toward the Sprint Goal** and **adapt the Sprint Backlog** as necessary, **adjusting the upcoming planned work**[8]. In other words, create a plan for the next 24 hours[9]. How you do it is open to the team to decide and implement.

This is a good time to **reinforce few key messages** to address few myths, poor practices and anti-patterns:

1. The Daily Scrum is **not** a Status meeting.
    a. Those used to traditional models may consider this event as a Status Meeting, where the team provides a status to the Product Owner or Scrum Master. Nothing could be further from the truth.
    b. The goal is for the Development Team to plan, amongst themselves, how to best accomplish the Sprint Goal; by creating a Daily Plan for the upcoming work day.
2. The Scrum Master and Product Owner do **not** have to attend the Daily Scrum.
    a. The Scrum Master does not *drive* the 'meeting'
    b. The Scrum Master should let the Development Team own and 'drive' the event. He may facilitate 'parts' of the event, only when required
    c. The Scrum Master and Product Owner attend the event, if they have some work as reflected in the Sprint Backlog.
    d. They are encouraged to attend so that they can listen in, and are available to support the team when requested; or, respond to any

---

[8] Each formal Scrum event provides a formal 'Inspect and Adapt point'. The *Inspect and Adapt* principle or practice should be applied continually, not just during formal events.

[9] 24 hours refers to the *period between two consecutive Daily Scrum events* (the actual working hours will be less than 8; with 6 hours being the permissible norm, with 2 hours accounting for 'overheads' not directly associated with development)

questions that the team may have, e.g., clarification of requirements; or request for support to resolve a blocker.

3. The Daily Scrum is **not** the only opportunity to inspect and adapt the plan; or communicate with each other.

   a. Team members can and should get together as often as required; however, the whole team does not need to meet repeatedly during the course of the day. As required, team may get together in *two's, or three's,* to discuss any specific issue or topic.

   b. Members of the Development Team should strike a balance between *maximizing time for individual work* Vs *maximizing time collaborating.*

4. The Scrum Master is **not** the only Scrum team member responsible for removing impediments, inhibitors and blockers.

   a. As part of a **self-managed** or **self-organized** team, *Development Team* members are themselves responsible for addressing impediments, issues or blockers, whenever possible.

   b. When team members believe it is beyond their *capacity* (as in 'bandwidth') or *ability* to resolve these themselves, they call upon the Scrum Master for immediate help.

   c. The Scrum Master will then attempt to resolve the impediments and blockers at the *earliest* instance; with the help of other partners such as the Product Owner or Managers, if required.

During the Sprint, team develops software incrementally. This may require *iterative* design, development, and testing, **in the Sprint itself**. The team is expected to complete few stories every two or three days. This is possible if the stories are small or 'right-sized'. Whenever possible, few team members may work on a single Story and complete it sooner. This approach is called **swarming**[10]. Completion of few stories, every two or three days, results in a smooth burndown of pending work. Teams must avoid delivering all the work at, or near, the very end of the Sprint.

---

[10] This notion is derived from behavior of Bees. Few bees tend to swarm on to a single flower to collect nectar from the same flower; while other bees swarm on other flowers, in groups. Together, they all complete their work in an optimal manner.

The penultimate event in the Sprint is the **Sprint Review**. It is the *Inspect and Adapt* point for the ***Sprint outcome*** *or results*; particularly, the *Increment aka Product Increment*, typically via a Demo. Key stakeholders inspect the product increment and provide feedback. The team must accept and incorporate the feedback, if there is value. Many teams prefer to conduct 'mini-Demos' two or more times in a Sprint, depending on the Sprint duration. This helps to avoid surprises towards the end of the Sprint, and provides an ability for critical or urgent feedback to be provided sooner. Enhancements could be made, based on this feedback, if there is value in doing so, during the same Sprint. However, even if the Demo is conducted earlier and there is time available before the Sprint ends, it is not necessary that this feedback has to be incorporated in the same Sprint. Feedback with highest priority or value may be incorporated at the earliest opportunity, in the same or next iteration. Sometimes, the scope of Review may encompass a work-in-process artifact, such as a User Interface Design, if feedback from stakeholders is required or desired.

The last event in the Sprint, the **Sprint Retrospective**, is the *Inspect and Adapt* point for individuals, interactions, processes, tools, and the *Definition of Done*; but, primarily, the *team* and the *process,* in real practice. The team is expected to embrace and build upon what went well; and identify opportunities to improve where things did not go so well. These could be in terms of *individual's* or *team's attitude and behavior,* or *team dynamics*; or some element in the *process* or *team's working environment*. Usually, these observations would result in the development of an improvement plan with a few action items; or an update to the Team's Working Agreement, and the Definitions of Ready or Done.

There are many Retrospective Games, or Retrospective formats, which the team can select from. The *Speedcar, Sailboat, Starfish, 4 L's (Liked, Lacked, Learned, Longed For), Start-Stop-Continue, Rose-Bud-Thorn, Mad-Glad-Sad, Keep-Add-More-Less (KALM)* are few popular approaches. These 'games' help to make this event interesting, engaging and effective.

Typically, at the end of the Sprint, the code is either released to the Production environment; or parked in an interim staging environment, until a 'whole package' can be released. This usually depends on whether a *new product is being developed* or whether *enhancements are being made to an existing product*. We will be discussing this aspect a little bit more in subsequent sections.

Organizations have already adopted, or are actively adopting, the DevOps and Continuous Integration/Continuous Deployment (CI/CD) models and methodologies to make this process streamlined.

Figure 2.2: Basics of the Scrum Framework

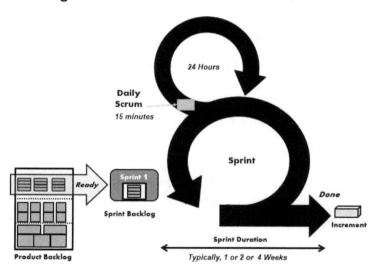

To summarize, Agile Frameworks, methodologies and models are either based on, or exhibit, the following characteristics:

- Application of Agile principles and values
- Focused on people and their interactions – collaboration and communication or 'conversations'
- Simple processes (*Minimum Viable Bureaucracy*) and reduction of Complexity
- Applies well to Complex Adaptive Systems
- Focused on *Values* and *Outcomes*, not *Outputs*
- *Incremental* and *iterative* in nature
- Focused on *optimization*, **not** *maximization*, of Efforts – there's value in work NOT done; most solutions are elegant, in their simplicity
- Reduction or elimination of Waste
- Based on *empirical* evidence, data and experience, rather than on theory and pure logic; verifiable by observation
- Prototyping, Experimentation and Validation; *Fail Fast* and move to the next Iteration
- Requirements, Architecture and Design may constantly evolve

Teams, which implement Agile models possess, exhibit and promote the following characteristics:

- Self-organized or self-managed, and cross-functional teams
- Small, highly collaborating teams with effective communications
- Deliver working software frequently
- Embrace Change, but Prioritize
- Constantly, Inspect and Adapt

The above characteristics are embodied in the Agile Principles, Values and Best Practices. Relevant details are presented in subsequent sections or chapters.

Chapter 2: The Agile Manifesto and Agile Values

The *Manifesto for Agile Software Development*, more commonly known as the *Agile Manifesto* was conceived, developed and adopted by seventeen software development thought leaders at the OOPSLA conference: Kent Beck, Mike Beedle, Arie van Bennekum, Alistair Cockburn, Ward Cunningham, Martin Fowler, James Grenning, Jim Highsmith, Andrew Hunt, Ron Jeffries, Jon Kern, Brian Marick, Robert C. Martin, Steve Mellor, Ken Schwaber, Jeff Sutherland, and Dave Thomas.

The Manifesto was the outcome of a desire to develop a 'lightweight' framework for software development, which could be used effectively by organizations across the world. It helps to minimize the bureaucracy and rigidity of existing models and be focused on outcomes instead of outputs. More emphasis was made on people, their interaction and collaboration; than on structures, hierarchies and boundaries. The Manifesto itself is shown in Table 2.1, in a slightly modified, tabular form to emphasize the 'Agile Values'. Each phrase, which is specified on the left side of the table below, is considered to be one of the **four** Agile Values. More information on the *Agile Manifesto* is available at: https://agilemanifesto.org/

Table 2.1: The Agile Manifesto

The Agile Manifesto

We are uncovering better ways of developing software by doing it and helping others do it. Through this work we have come to value:

Individuals and interactions	over	processes and tools
Working software	over	comprehensive documentation
Customer collaboration	over	contract negotiation
Responding to change	over	following a plan

That is, while there is value in the items on the right,
we value the items on the left more.

The *first* Agile Value lies in the emphasis on **interacting and collaborating individuals**, rather than on *processes or tools*. During software development, in the appropriate context, team members should strike a *balance* between *working individually* and *together as a part of the team*. On a day-to-day basis, each team member plans how to optimize the time taken to complete his or her own work, while spending some time interacting effectively with others. Frequent interactions are required to discuss and resolve a problem; or review a requirement, design, or solution. If possible, team members should interact regularly to help each other or those outside the team.

Processes and Tools **are** required, but should not be allowed to become inhibitors. If Jira or the Jenkins pipeline is 'down', work still needs to get done. Teams should find effective means to achieve progress towards *completion of any pending work*, or *valuable interactions*, such as team-building exercises or just 'fun time'. Processes and Tools play a supportive role. When system tools are not available, whiteboards, pen and paper are very effective tools. A *Minimum Viable Bureaucracy* is required to avoid chaos and bring some sense of discipline, without undermining flexibility, creativity, and innovation. To avoid antipatterns, we must be able to distinguish between *Being Agile* and *Being Chaotic*[11].

The second value is the focus on **working software**. Everything the team does is focused on developing highly *valuable*, *working* software that will *delight customers*. It is quite possible that a team does **not** deliver working software at the end of every iteration, or Sprint. However, if the work is scoped 'right', through User Stories with small sizes, it is possible to deliver working software at the end of every Sprint.

Documentation is important; but *'how much'* or *'how little'* should be left to individual teams (**not** individuals), within the broad organizational framework (aka standards and best practices). Teams should include broad or specific guidance in their **Team Working Agreement,** to provide a common understanding on *documentation best practices*. Increasingly, organizations and teams are leveraging on Wikis and Confluence instead of traditional document repositories to enhance **transparency**, which is one of the three **Scrum 'Pillars'**. Traditional document repositories tend to have few undesirable characteristics, which include performance issues, restrictive access management, and

---

[11] Per Dave Thomas: I see some teams that use the word "agile" when they really mean "chaotic"

lack of visibility. There is a need for **Information Radiators** rather than **Information Refrigerators**.

The *third* value relates to **collaboration with customers** vis-à-vis contract negotiations. Contracts are involved if an organization either *sells their products and services* to their customers and/or *employs suppliers to provide them with certain products and services*. In both cases, collaboration is more important than the contract negotiation itself. This can be best illustrated with a personal, real life example below.

A few years back, I led a software development project, which entailed building a custom online solution, leveraging an existing platform of a successful Fintech company. Due to complexity of the *'legal and compliance'* processes at the organization I worked at, i.e., the customer, there were repeated delays in the closing of the contract. Whenever the contract was ready to be signed by the customer, inevitably, someone would recommend that few changes be made to the contract. This required another round of review and approval by the Legal and Compliance departments. The situation was compounded by the fact that the vendor did not have sufficient experience with: (a) Agile models for software development and delivery; and (b) drawing up contracts for Agile projects. As a result, the scope of work and timelines were constantly changing during the course of the project. Even by the time we completed the project, the contract had not yet been signed off.

By applying this Agile value, we were successful in developing a *sense of trust and collaboration* between the two companies. The incomplete or evolving contract, with ongoing negotiations, did not prove to be a show-stopper or an obstacle to the team's development and delivery process. If each party is engaged in a win-win situation, collaboration always trumps negotiation by one party for a 'better' deal.

The *fourth*, and final, *Agile Value* is the focus on a team's **ability to respond to change** vis-à-vis a *Plan*. Change can manifest in terms of changing requirements or scope, schedule and funding/cost as well as changing circumstances, both within and outside the control of the organization, or the team. Teams should embrace valuable and meaningful changes.

If we remember that the solution is being developed for a customer, with the intent of delighting the customer, we should always elicit and incorporate customer feedback. This is significantly important. Accepting change does not mean we have to incorporate it right away. Nor does it mean that we have to accept feedback, which provides little value. We should be able to assess competing priorities and develop a plan, which makes the most sense; and, the plan itself could and must change, if required.

A plan is a plan…is a plan…is a plan, however 'foolproof' it is. It can never be 100% 'complete', 'correct', 'accurate'; because it is generally based on very little upfront knowledge and foresight. This knowledge or foresight decreases exponentially with the length, or duration, of the plan horizon. Minute details in a five-year plan may actually be useless, but a high-level, milestone-based five-year plan could be quite helpful. Nonetheless, in the Agile world, planning for shorter horizons is desired. The primary purpose of the Daily Scrum is for the Development Team to plan for the next day, based on the progress made on the plan for the previous day. See Figure 2.3 for *Agile Planning* at various plan horizons.

Figure 2.3: Agile Planning

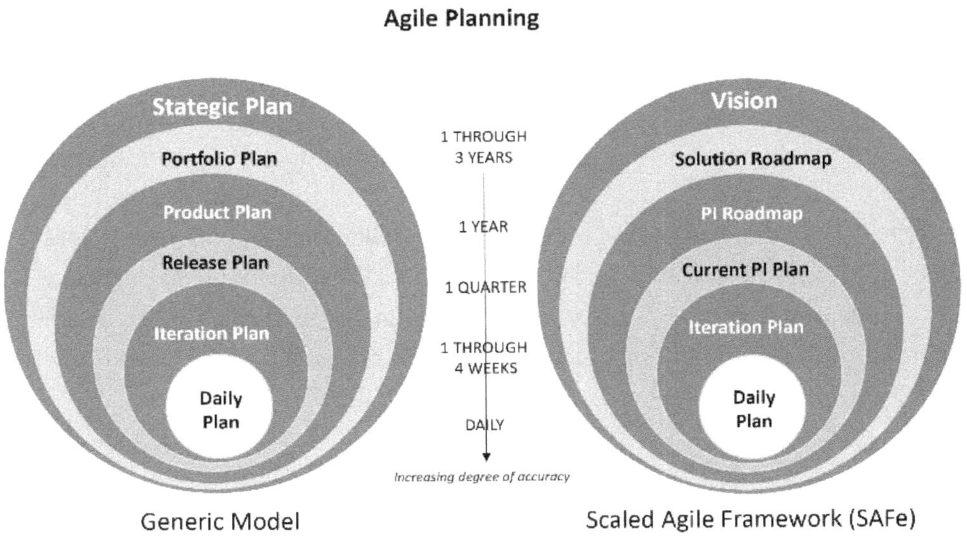

Agile Planning

Generic Model   Scaled Agile Framework (SAFe)

The most accurate plan is the **Daily Plan**, developed during the *Daily Scrum*. It is prepared in the overall context of the **Iteration or Sprint Plan**, which is developed during the *Sprint Planning* event, at the beginning of the Sprint.

Most organizations develop a *quarterly* plan as well. Organizations implementing the SAFe model call this the **Program Increment (PI) Plan**. Several teams working on the *same Product*, get together over a day or two in a 'big room', to discuss and arrive at this Plan. This event is referred to as *PI Planning*, or sometimes, *Big Room Planning*.

The **Release Plan** usually refers to a *longer-term* plan, which may extend over several quarters; and, sometimes, over a year or two. It is associated with the release of a *new* **Version** of the product. Few organizations may distinguish between *Major* or *Minor Versions*, such as 1.0, 1.1, 1.2, ..., 2.0, 2.1, 2.2 and so on. In such cases, each Major or Minor Version would have its own Release Plan. In other words, the Release Plan is associated with *any* Release, for any major or minor versions. The released version of the product may constitute a *Minimum Releasable Product (MRP)* or *Minimum Releasable Feature (MRF)*; or, *Minimum Marketable Product (MMP)* or *Minimum Marketable Feature (MMF)*; or, even a *Minimum Viable Product (MVP)*.

The *Minimum Viable Product (MVP)* is the *minimum set of features* being released to a limited set of customers or prospects to **test** its viability or usefulness to the customer. The term *Viability* also refers to the 'completeness' of the product being released, to serve as one functional unit. If any 'piece' is missing, the customer doesn't get a 'complete' experience and the value of the product may be considered low. Once the test results are received and evaluated, the organization may then consider the same set (or an updated set) of features to be released to all the customers and prospects. This is the *Minimum Releasable Product (MRP)*. The organization could release the product in batches of Features, each of which could be a *Minimum Releasable Feature (MRF)*. These releasable features or products become *Marketable* if the organization has considered the demand or marketability, and probability of adoption, which will determine the success or failure of the product.

All these plans are prepared under a broader **Product or Solution Roadmap**, which typically spans 1-3 years. In recent years, longer term planning is being strongly discouraged; and few proponents or organizations believe that a *Product Roadmap is not actually required*. This may be *somewhat* true in the context of Agile software development and delivery, if the requirements, priorities and needs are constantly changing. Nonetheless, business leaders need to continue **strategic planning** in order to successfully meet or fulfill the organization's vision, mission, strategies, objectives and goals.

The **Three Horizons Framework** provides great perspectives for Strategic Planning in the *product development* context. Product Managers and Leadership, including Business and Portfolio Managers, need to plan for longer plan horizons. Typically, the duration of each horizon ranges from 3-5 years.

Horizon One represents **existing or core businesses**, particularly, its *cash cows*. The organization must *defend and grow* its most profitable products and services to continue to maximize revenues, profits, and cash flows.

Horizon Two is associated with **emerging opportunities**, which the organization has identified based on its strengths. These opportunities would provide substantial returns but would require *significant investments*. *Fast mover* organizations that successfully leverage these opportunities are poised to become market leaders, if they are not already so.

Horizon Three signifies potential opportunities associated with **innovation, research and development**. Sufficient investment should be made in these risky opportunities if the organizations wishes to lead the market from the forefront, in the near future.

For more details, please visit:

https://www.mckinsey.com/business-functions/strategy-and-corporate-finance/our-insights/enduring-ideas-the-three-horizons-of-growth

Chapter 3: Agile Principles

The *Agile Principles* should *influence*, if not *determine*, various aspects of the organization's Agile model and its culture, as well as the team's day-to-day practices, behavior and culture. The principles are self-explanatory, but it is quite important to *very clearly* understand the original intent; whether the principles themselves or their interpretation have evolved over time; and how they relate to development of an Agile thinking, culture and best practices.

Table 2.2: The Agile Principles

#	The Agile Principles
1	Our highest priority is to *satisfy the customer* through early and continuous delivery of valuable software.
2	*Welcome changing requirements*, even late in development. Agile processes harness change for the customer's competitive advantage.
3	*Deliver working software frequently*, from a couple of weeks to a couple of months, with a preference to the shorter timescale.
4	Business people and developers must *work together* daily throughout the project
5	Build projects around *motivated individuals*. Give them the environment and *support* they need, and *trust* them to get the job done.
6	The most efficient and effective method of conveying information to and within a development team is *face-to-face conversation*
7	*Working software* is the primary measure of progress
8	Agile processes promote *sustainable development*. The sponsors, developers, and users should be able to maintain a constant pace indefinitely.
9	Continuous attention to *technical excellence* and *good design* enhances agility
10	*Simplicity*—the art of maximizing the amount of work not done—is essential.
11	The best architectures, requirements, and designs emerge from *self-organizing teams*
12	At regular intervals, the team *reflects* on how to become more effective, then *tunes and adjusts* its behavior accordingly

Table 2.3 shows a simplified view of the Agile Principles: the major and implicit *focus* of each *Principle*.

Table 2.3: Focus of the Agile Principles

#	Primary Focus	Implicit Focus
1	Satisfy the Customer	Continuous Delivery of Business Value
2	Welcome Change	Enhance Customer's Competitive Advantage
3	Deliver Frequently	Shorter Iterations
4	Work Together	Collaboration of Business and Technology stakeholders
5	Motivated individuals	Trust and Support
6	Face-to-face Conversation	Effective Communications
7	Measure Progress (Metrics)	Working Software
8	Sustainable Development	Constant Pace (Velocity)
9	Technical Excellence	Good Design
10	Maintain Simplicity	Maximizing work not done
11	Self-organizing teams	Emerging architectures, requirements, and designs
12	Reflect and Adjust	Inspect & Adapt (Retrospectives)

Details, context and application of each Principle is provided in Part 3 of this book. The actual *Agile Principles,* as originally specified, are available at:

https://agilemanifesto.org/principles.html

Chapter 4: Scrum Values

The **Scrum** framework has also specified _its own Values_: **Courage, Focus, Commitment, Respect, and Openness**. A poster, which describes these Values may be downloaded from: https://www.scrum.org/resources/scrum-values-poster.

Figure 2.4: The Scrum Values

Source and Copyright: Scrum.org

While the poster shown above provides an adequate description of the values, we may draw few more inferences for each of these values.

COURAGE

Essentially, this implies that team members should have the courage to do the 'right' thing; accept challenges, and work on tough problems, rather than take the easy way out. *Remember Occam's Razor though: Sometimes, the simplest explanation is the usually the right one; and the simplest way out may be the most optimal one. Most situations do not require unnecessary complications.*

Courage also implies that team members should also speak up when required: ask questions and present their opinions. Very often, team members remain silent, either thinking they may be asking a silly question, or that someone may get offended. Firstly, there's never a silly question. When someone asks a question, it doesn't reflect 'ignorance' but an intention to learn more about the subject being discussed. This is not a bad thing, since we should constantly strive to learn about what we don't know. It may be quite detrimental, or even dangerous, to make an *incorrect assumption*, even if it appears implicit; or make an *incorrect conclusion*, without clarifying a doubt you may have. It may result in an *incorrect* assessment, documentation and implementation of the requirements, design or code, leading to the development of a poor-quality product.

Secondly, it is perfectly acceptable to disagree with a team member, but without being disagreeable. Team norms should be established through continual discussions, and documented in the *Team Working Agreement*. Team members who are introverts, and are reticent in discussions, should be encouraged to speak up and participate more actively. All team members are equal – there's no hierarchy – even if there is a *Lead* role. If there is indeed a *first amongst equals* Lead role, it should be shared; and Team members may continually take turns to perform this role. This ensures that everyone on the team gets an opportunity to maximize his contribution or participation; and continually develop his or her communication and leadership skills. Everyone should get a chance to share or perform any responsibility, wherever and whenever possible.

Finally, a team member may remain silent due to peripheral distractions, or while multitasking. While this behavior has no relation to 'courage', Scrum Master may need to probe further to determine the cause. This will help to prevent individuals developing undesirable behaviors, which may result in anti-patterns.

FOCUS

It is very important to have a *laser-sharp focus* on the *team goals* and *work at hand*. There are several reasons for this. Firstly, there is a 'limited' duration of the Sprint, within which the goal is to be achieved. Secondly, with lack of focus, team members may become stuck in *analysis paralysis* and get very little done. Finally, it is very easy to get distracted when working alone, or in isolation. Agile principles and practices actively promote self-organization, self-discipline, ownership, accountability and responsibility. Team members should be able to develop and maintain focus without the intervention or oversight of the Scrum Master, Leads or Managers.

COMMITMENT

In the Agile world, Commitment is a *value* not an *act*. The team does not necessarily need to *commit, as an act,* to deliver a particular quantum of work, say, worth 50 story points. The team may *plan* to achieve the target of 50 points, and be fully committed to it. Whether the team achieves the target, or not, may depend on external factors that the team has no control on. Sometimes, it is the result of *'environment issues'*: the development, testing and deployment environments are 'down' or unavailable. In other cases, it may be due to *external dependencies*. Nonetheless, the team should strive to minimize the negative impact of controllable factors. The team needs to analyze and resolve dependencies, well ahead of the iteration, to avoid adverse impacts of unresolved dependencies on the active iteration. Organizations and teams, which have yet to fully 'mature', may insist upon the use of 'commitment', in terms of a committed quantum of work during each iteration. This behavior and expectation should be discouraged.

The notions of *'Committed* Story Points' and 'Completed Story Points' in Jira may have propagated the misconception about 'Commitment'. A tool like Jira should not influence our understanding of 'Commitment'. If we do, it is akin to putting the cart before the horse. Jira constitutes one of the *means* for supporting the team's performance, and not the 'end'. The team does *not* exist to support Jira, but Jira exists to support the team.

RESPECT

'Give respect and get respect'. In practice, we often respect those who are perceived as the 'smarter' team members – the performers or the 'more qualified' members – as compared to others, who are considered 'less qualified'. This behavior is not conducive to building an effective and highly performing team. All team members are equal, which means we must respect each one. We must respect their individuality and strive to help them grow and be effective contributors to the team. Also, we can earn or gain respect only if we respect them. In reality, respect is always earned; so, team members should continuously strive to earn and gain respect by doing the 'right' things in the 'right' way.

OPENNESS

Team members and other stakeholders must be frank and forthright with each other. **Transparency** is one of the three Scrum Pillars (the other two being **Inspection** and **Adaptation**). This helps everyone to be 'on the same page', to eliminate or reduce surprises, risks and issues. It encompasses sharing of information, which facilitates effective discussions and decision-making. *Openness* and *transparency* help to build trust and respect for each other; thereby, maximizing the probability of team's or organization's success. These values enhance interpersonal relations as well as inter-team or cross-functional collaboration.

Implicit, in these *five* Scrum values, is the *sixth* but informal value: **TRUST**. It goes hand-in-hand with *RESPECT*; and constitutes the foundation on which various other values are based. Without *Trust* amongst team members, it is very difficult to teams to become effective or high-performing.

Figure 2.5: Trust - the Implicit Value

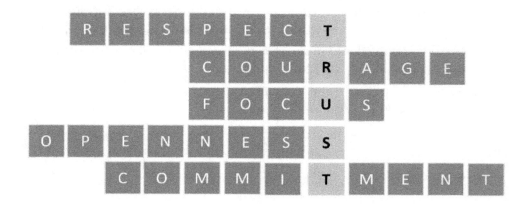

There are a few other 'informal' or implicit values we could consider. Team Members, Managers and Servant Leaders should encourage behaviors that will make the team feel **SAFE.** *FEAR* is considered the biggest enemy of Agile teams. It is the opposite of COURAGE. Leaders should nurture an environment and culture that is free from retaliation, discouragement and ridicule. Team members should be encouraged to *OPEN* up and participate actively in team activities. Finally, work should be **FUN**. Team members should look forward to working at the office; and to *work together* rather than in isolation.

Another implicit value I would like to highlight is **BALANCE**. Development of *norms* lead to **NORMAL** expectations, attitudes and behavior. Figure 2.6 below indicates a few Normal Distributions, which may be applied to various situations. The peak of each curve may be considered to represent a *tipping point* or *point of equilibrium or balance*. If we consider the right side to represent desired behavior or outcomes (e.g., High Quality), the curve will skew heavily to the right until the *Theory of Marginal Utility* kicks in. Any improvement beyond this point may result is unnecessary risks, insufficient rewards, or excessive costs and overheads. Teams should always develop norms such that there is always an optimal balance between two extremes. Team actions and behavior should fall within an *acceptable range* on both sides of this equilibrium point, without stretching too far out to the extremes, at either end.

Figure 2.6: The Normal Curve

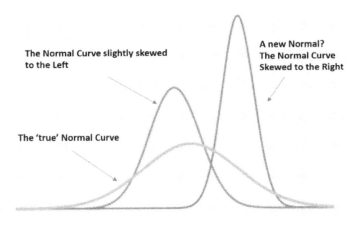

Source: Adapted from a picture in STAT 88, a textbook authored by Ani Adhikari, and is available at
http://stat88.org/textbook/notebooks/Chapter_08/02_Standard_Normal_Curve.html

Part 3: Agile Principles and Best Practices

This part of the book helps the reader understand *each* principle and how best practices are based on the underlying principles. Please note that the focus is on understanding the principles better. As a result, descriptions of the underlying best practices may not be as detailed as you may desire. Please refer to other books, in particular, the Field Guide, for more detailed information.

Chapter 1: The Principle of Customer Satisfaction

'Our highest priority is to satisfy the customer through early and continuous delivery of valuable software'.

The Customer is King. Yes, the customer is *indeed* the King. If we forget this age-old adage, an organization's very existence is at stake. Organizations, including market leaders, may quickly fade into oblivion if they become complacent and lose sight of this focus. A business exists *only* because of its customers; and, this is very important to remember while performing our tasks.

Every effort that we make, as a member of an Agile Software Development team, is to ensure that we *maximize the value of the software* we develop and it *delights the customer*. We build software for the customer and not for own self-actualization. We do not need to spend an extraordinary amount of time to make our software 'perfect'. There's *elegance in simplicity* and *work NOT done is very important*. We should eliminate all bells and whistles. Nonetheless, quality of the software we develop has to be very high. We need to build the 'right' software in the 'right' way. Seeking what is 'right' is a continuous endeavor for the organization, as well as Agile teams.

To be able to meet customer needs, in a timely manner, we have to **develop and deliver software in small increments**. The sooner we meet the needs, the better it is. At the very least, we should deliver what *organizational* customers have asked for, **in time**, for them to leverage market demands before the trends shift away.

At this point, it is important to distinguish between **Sprints** and **Releases**, even though these are intricately connected. In an ideal case, each Sprint will culminate in a Release. In practice, this depends on several factors:

- **Nature of the work being done**: Are the teams working on enhancing an existing software; or, are they involved in new product development?
- **The organization's infrastructure and processes**: Is the CI/CD pipeline fully automated? Is testing completely automated? Does the software (increment) meet the **Release** *Definition of Done (DoD)?* Does the organization truly implement *Continuous Deployment?*

- **Value of the delivered software:** Will release of the software developed by the group of Agile teams (or, each individual team), in each Sprint, yield sufficient value to the customer?

The *Scrum Guide* does not elaborate much on the *Release* aspect of software development or delivery. It focuses on the *potential releasability* of the software, delivered after every Sprint. The Guide referred to the software as a *Potentially Shippable or Releasable **Product Increment***; now, commonly referred to as '**Increment**'. This *increment* may be the software delivered by a single team, or a number of teams working in concert. The Release decision is deferred to the organization, and it is usually based on the following considerations:

- Most Agile teams should be able to release the Increment after every Sprint, if they are part of the *same Release train*; and *their inter-dependencies* have been fully addressed, so that the *sum total of their individual increments* meet the *Release DoD*.
- Teams enhancing *existing software* will be able to release the Increment after every Sprint, if the Increment provides an immediate *value* to the customer
- Teams engaged in *new product development* will have to wait until their product meets the MVP/MRP/MMP requirements
- If *testing* can be fully automated, and all *checks and balances* (previously called *Entry or Exit Criteria*) can be fully automated, the Increment can be released *automatically*, without human interventions. These checks and balances refer to successful completion of *reviews;* and *'rules'*, which must be satisfied. Only then, can the code be promoted from a lower Pre-Prod environment all the way through to the Production Environment.

To summarize, each increment must have some value to the customer in order to be considered for a Release. Value could imply a simpler way of doing something that an end-customer or user currently struggles with, i.e., a better customer experience. Alternatively, it could entail a more aesthetic color scheme, or the resolution of an issue such as a 'production defect'. Even resolving a simple issue, such as 'browser timeout' or a 'perpetually spinning progress bar', could have a lot of value to the customer. Small value-based increments can be deployed continuously while enhancing an existing software.

As mentioned earlier, it may not be possible to *always* deploy software in *small* increments, i.e., deliver to the customer, if the team is developing and launching **new software**. In such cases, the team or organization needs to focus on a ***Minimum Releasable Feature (MRF)*** or a ***Minimum Releasable Product (MRP).*** Normally, marketability is a major consideration, and the organization or team should focus on a ***Minimum Marketable Feature (MMF)*** or a ***Minimum Marketable Product (MMP).*** Two aspects to consider, to understand these terms better, are:

- The product constitutes a set of features
- You may be able release a product, but it may not always be marketable i.e., the customer may not be interested in using it or paying for it.

In order to increase the product's marketability and value, organizations may consider the MVP approach. Most people consider the term '**Minimum Viable Product (MVP)**' to be the same as any one of the terms described above. This is not correct. MVP refers to a *product*, i.e., a *minimum set of features*, released to *select customers* for *experimentation* or *test marketing*. First, you develop a hypothesis or hypotheses; then, build the MVP; then, release it as a pilot; and, finally, validate your hypotheses. If your hypotheses were correct, you may launch it as an MRP or MMP to all your customers. This could include or *exclude functionality or features*, based on feedback acquired during the experiment. If any hypothesis proved to be false, partially or completely, you need to 'fix' the software to meet actual market needs.

Perhaps, the most important aspect of Agile Software Development is **Customer Value**. In order to maximize this, organizations and teams have to *continuously, or continually, get customer feedback;* and *adapt the increment or next iteration* of the software accordingly. It is preferred to get feedback directly from customers. If that is difficult, or not possible, you may want to listen to the *Voice of the Customer (VOC)*. This usually is gathered from organizational stakeholders, who interface directly with customers, such as Customer Support or Sales Reps. The Marketing organization may gather feedback through Surveys and other means; sometimes, through third-party agencies. Nowadays, various mechanisms enable organizations to track and gather User data or analytics. However, with the increasing trend toward empowering Users to control their own data, through various Privacy laws, this option may suffice sometimes, but not always.

It is very difficult to identify or quantify *Customer Value*. Designers and Developers may be very excited about a 'great' feature; but teams need to check if the customer will be equally enthusiastic. Or, the Product team may be very sure that the documented requirements appropriately represent real customer needs. None of these may be true, and all assumptions must be validated in some practical way.

Customer Value may not necessarily be the same as **Business Value**. Anything that an organization does must have some *discrete* business value; otherwise, it is not worth doing. A valid exception i.e., *when an organization does not seek Business Value,* applies only in the case of a charitable or non-profit organization. Otherwise, Customer Value must be fully aligned to Business Value. Without this alignment, Customer value may come at an unreasonable cost.

We should *first* try to identify customer value in a suitable way, at the 'level' of Epics or Features. For instance, ask: *what is the value of an 'auto-pay' feature for a credit card? How does the value of this feature relate to value of other features?*

One common way to 'measure' value is a kind of *Bubble Sort*: assign a score to a *benchmarked* or *baselined* feature; and then assign value to other features based on this reference point. The feature with the highest score is placed on top. Starting at the top of a list, evaluate the value of a Feature vis-à-vis the Baseline; then, repeat, till the last feature on the list is evaluated. Others follow a more 'sophisticated approach', such as *Weighted Shortest Job First (WSJF),* which is based on *Cost of Delay*. There are many ways to 'measure' value. However, we must understand that all of these are based on some conventions or assumptions, which may neither be accurate nor precise. For instance, we may not be able to accurately determine the Cost of Delay, for either individual Features or the product itself. Nonetheless, having a 'measure' of value is better than having nothing at all. At the very least, it will help teams to prioritize their work.

Determining customer value at Story level – User Story or 'Technical Story' – is even more difficult. Any such attempt may lead to confusion; and may often yield fallacious measures or assumptions. Teams may find that it is not worth spending a *significant* amount of time or effort on this endeavor.

Teams should not engage in this endeavor just for the act of 'measuring value', or because the process so demands. In short, ask yourself *if the team is getting any value* in trying to determine business value or customer value for a Feature, Epic, or Story. Intuitively, without any formal process, you may be able to determine that few Features or Stories have little or no customer value. These should be assigned very *low priority or zero value;* and should not be worked on, if possible.

Few ways of determining Business Value at the *Portfolio level* include: *Breakeven Analysis, Cost Benefit Ratio, Return on Investment (RoI), Cash Flow Analysis, Real Options Analysis,* and *Net Present Value.* All of these approaches require an analysis using *formal methodologies,* and are based on *financial data or projections.* It may however be noted that most of these financial values are *guesstimates,* and there may be a fairly high degree of subjectivity. In addition, these *forecasts* are based on historical data. The past may not *always* be a good indicator of the future. Nonetheless, using *few measures or KPIs* at the *Portfolio level* is better than not using one at all. Those interested in learning more about Business Value can find additional information at:

https://www.slideshare.net/GervaisJohnson/agile-business-value

Business Value determination at the *portfolio level* is aimed at analyzing *what is worth doing* and *what is not.* Epics or Features, which provide the most returns are ranked at the top and considered worth pursuing. At the *program or team level,* these scores help in *prioritization* of Features, Epics or Stories.

Table 3.1 provides few common ways of determining Business Value at the Program or Team levels. These include the following approaches: Bubble Sort, MoSCoW, Kano, WSJF, NPS, etc. Detailed analysis of these approaches is provided in other books in this series, e.g., the Field Guide.

These approaches are best applied to *prioritization of Epics and/or Features,* but can be applied to stories as well. These approaches usually start with some *qualitative analysis* of the Feature (or Epic or Story), which are then ranked, based on some *quantitative measure* assigned to each of them.

Table 3.1: Select Business Value Models

#	Level	Approach	Description
1	Epics or Features	Bubble Sort	Rank order *Epics or Features* from Top to Bottom of Backlog (stories with higher business value is placed on the top) by continually shuffling the stories, prior to PI Planning
2	Stories	Bubble Sort	Rank order *Stories* from Top to Bottom of Backlog (stories with higher business value is placed on the top) by continually shuffling the stories, prior to Sprint Planning
3	Epics or Features	MoSCoW	Identify *Epics or Features* as Must Do, Should Do, Could Do, Won't Do; usually, very early in the Backlog management process – well before PI Planning
4	Epics or Features	Kano	Identify Epics or Features as Must-be Quality, One-dimensional Quality, Attractive Quality, Indifferent Quality, and Reverse Quality; usually, stated as Satisfiers, Dissatisfiers or Exciters depending on perceived Quality – well before PI Planning
5	Epics or Features	Net Promoter Score (NPS)	Identifying Promoters, Detractors, and Passives from Customer Feedback (typically, Surveys) and computing NPS score, from score assigned by customer to the question or factor – well before PI Planning
6	Epics or Features	Weighted Shortest Job First (WSJF)	Computed as a Ratio of *Cost of Delay* to *Job Duration (or Size)*. It is based on the premise that knowledge of *Cost of Delay* leads to better prioritization or job sequencing, as compared to any model based on theoretical ROI – well before PI Planning

Chapter 2: The Principle of Embracing Change

'Welcome changing requirements, even late in development. Agile processes harness change for the customer's competitive advantage'.

Almost everyone who has been involved in software development projects, particularly, in some Project Management role, would have heard about the **'Iron Triangle'** or the **three constraints of *Scope*, *Time (or, Schedule)* and *Cost***. Most would agree that successful project management requires a delicate balance amongst these three factors. Projects executed using the Waterfall methodology have failed, or achieved limited success, due to the following factors:

- *Scope Creep*: Project scope changes frequently due to one or more reasons: requirements change; new discovery invalidates old assumptions; there are 'too many' change requests, and so on.
- *Cost Overruns*: Initial cost estimates do not hold good over an extended period of time. Very often, we underestimate the resource requirements during initial planning. We are almost always 'over budget'.
- *Delays*: Planning, however sophisticated, is perhaps doomed for failure if plans are made for a period that extends beyond a quarter. The degree of accuracy of any plan declines exponentially with the duration of the plan horizon. Daily Plans are more accurate than weekly plan, which in turn are more accurate than monthly plans, and so on.

Whenever we have 'problems' with delays or cost overruns, the natural tendency is to *control scope creep*. We tend to forget that the primary objective of the project is to *deliver software that meets customer needs*. Instead, we are focused on executing a 'successful' project by meeting arbitrarily set deadlines. We shut ourselves out from any kind of *customer feedback or change requests*. We implement elaborate *Change Management processes,* which discourage adoption of any kind of change. Even if we are 'successful' in completing the project 'in time', much to management's satisfaction, we are often 'surprised' to find that customer adoption or acceptance is much below expectations. In short, we lost sight of the project goal; and the project actually failed.

It is quite difficult to execute a project with *fixed scope, fixed schedule, and fixed cost*. The challenge is compounded when costs and schedules are 'fixed', but the scope creeps. The growing belief, amongst organizations globally, that the Waterfall methodology is not suitable for software development can be ascribed to the reasons described above.

I personally believe that we could successfully deliver projects using the Waterfall methodology *for shorter timeframes*. In fact, at one of the organizations I worked at, I palyed a key role in developing a methodology called *'Staggered Waterfall'* during the early 2000s. It essentially comprised of the same Waterfall phases – *Ideation and Discovery, Analysis and Design, Development and Testing, Deployment and Go Live* – but in an overlapping manner. We did not wait for 'perfection' in, or 'completion' of, any phase to begin the next one.

Once we had 'good enough' requirements, we started Analysis and Design for the first batch of requirements. Once we had 'sufficient' analysis and design done, we started development. Of course, like in any Waterfall project, we had fixed timelines for each project. Please see the Figure 3.1 below. As you may have realized, we had tweaked the organization's standard 'hybrid SDLC' [12] model to arrive at this methodology.

Over a period of time, most organizations started to realize that, despite 'successful' completion of projects, the value of the software being delivered was not as high, or as much, as expected. To address this issue, organizations started to encourage teams' ability to adopt change. There are many ways to be 'change-friendly', but we shall limit ourselves to the context of software development.

---

[12] At this organization, there were three standard Software Development Lifecycle (SDLC) models: Waterfall, Agile, and Hybrid. In the 2000-2005 timeframe, there were spiral or iterative models, but Scrum had not yet been adopted in a major way.

Figure 3.1: The Staggered Waterfall Model

The Staggered Waterfall Methodology

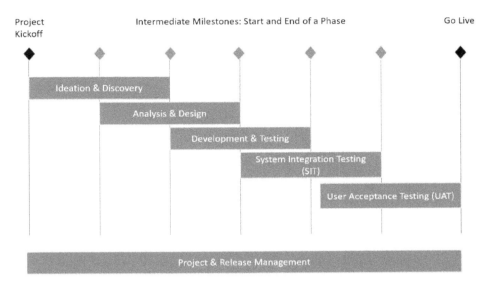

Changing Scope and Requirements

Once we acknowledge that *the only thing that is constant is change*, we are setting out on a path of success. Success as in an individual, success as in a team, and success as in an organization. We should not only be open to change but embrace it.

Due to the nature of the Agile model, some element of 'scope creep' is natural. When we start execution on an Epic, not 'everything' is known. We start only with the bits (or, 'bites') of what is known, which is encapsulated in a 'small story'. The remaining *requirement 'bits'* will get detailed and developed over a period of time. New discoveries may be made in the requirements, as they get detailed during the refinement process. Sometimes, details are uncovered during the design or development process. These may result in additional stories. This 'scope creep' can be monitored using Version Reports.

Version Reports are developed by organizing Epics and Stories into versions, for a specific release. Addition of new stories to the Epics in the version, over a period of time, may give an appearance of scope creep. The Version Reports, a type of a release burnup or burndown chart, indicates when the work on the version will be completed; and how progress on the Version is being made. This is based on the rate at which the work is being currently burned down. Version Reports are valuable when the Release spans across several Sprints, or several months.

Changing Costs and Schedules

In an 'Agile project', you <u>cannot</u> have a *fixed scope* and *fixed schedule*. One of these has to give. To illustrate this better, I will use a mathematical construct of *functions* and *variables*. The first formula, which is very intuitive, indicates that the **Probability** of *Success* depends on how well we manage *Scope*, *Schedule* and *Costs*. See Figure 3.2.

The second formula is more important, in our context, in order to understand *what depends on what*. In other words, which is the *dependent variable,* and which is the *independent variable*. These are important choices to make.

Figure 3.2: Dependent and Independent Variables

A Formula for Success

General formula: $Y = f(X)$

$$P(S) = f(a, b, c) \quad ... 1$$

Where
a = Scope
b = Schedule
c = Cost
S = Success
P = Probability

$$F(b) = f(a, c) \quad ... 2$$

As mentioned earlier, we should not consider a *fixed scope* as well as a *fixed schedule,* while planning and executing Agile projects. We should perhaps make the *Schedule* dependent on the *Scope*. In other words, we should allow for 'Scope Creep' or 'Changing Scope' or 'Change Requests' and allow *Schedule* to change accordingly. It is important to clarify that Schedule Change considerations may be analyzed from two perspectives: *Project timelines* and *Iteration* timelines.

From the **project timeline perspective**, it is recommended that:

- You define a *Minimum Releasable Product (MRP)* or *Minimum Releasable Feature (MRF);* or whatever is suitable: amongst *Features* or *Product, Releasable* or *Marketable*.
- Specify a *timeline* and allow it to move, within 'reasonable' limits, for *changing scope* e.g., extension of the timeline by a few months may be reasonable, *if the focus is on ensuring that delivered software (MRP) **will** have adequate or desired value*. Others may choose to drop MRP features and allow 'limited' change in the Schedule. This depends, primarily, on the balance you seek between *how soon* you want to product to reach the market vis-à-vis what is the *minimum feature set* that is valuable.

From an **Iteration perspective**, you do not have an *option to change the duration; but you do have control over the scope in the iteration.* A Sprint is timeboxed – you cannot change the duration depending on whether you are able to get things done sooner, or you need more time to complete the work planned.

The *only consideration* for allowing *scope change within* an *Active Sprint*, or iteration, tends to be based on the following:

- Last minute acceptance of a *request deemed critical*: needs to be urgently delivered sometime *during,* or *by the end of*, the Sprint .
- If the quantum of work is beyond the team's current capacity, *the team* should agree to *swap out* part of the already planned work. The team should try to accomplish this without impacting the Sprint goal, as much as possible.
- Very little or no risk and dependencies should be introduced in the Sprint.
- Such changes should be made on exceptional basis, rather than as a norm.

If it is difficult to incorporate changes within a Sprint, a suggested **normal** approach should be based the following considerations:

- Continually *prioritize changes* along with other items in the Backlog
- *Plan* to address changes as soon as possible - in the next Sprint, or subsequent Sprints.
- Treat changes at the *same priority* as other comparable 'regular' backlog items, such as a Stories or Defects. The best way to do this is to add the change requests as Stories or Epics, depending on the size, and prioritize like others

Finally, it is imperative to mention that our *customers' goals and objectives should be treated as if these were our own*. Enabling customers' success ensures our success. Our efforts, and delivered software, should enable our customers to develop and maintain a *competitive advantage*. We should deliver features that will enhance their *Unique Selling Propositions (USPs)*. Our delivery should always be frequent – quick and timely – so that our customers can take advantage of swiftly moving market opportunities, such as sudden spike in demand of their products and services. Being highly responsive to *customer needs* enhances *customer satisfaction*, *trust* and *repeat business*.

Chapter 3: The Principle of Delivering Frequently

'Deliver working software frequently, from a couple of weeks to a couple of months, with a preference to the shorter timescale'.

There are two aspects to this principle: *working software* and *shorter iterations*. We will discuss the first aspect elsewhere, and focus on the second, in this chapter.

One of the critical foundations of an Agile model or methodology is the concept of *iteration*, and its *duration*. In Scrum, iterations are called Sprints. Per the Scrum Guide, the maximum duration of a Sprint is a month, and shorter durations are preferred. This duration may be dependent on one or more of the following factors:

- How mature the organization is - in adopting and implementing Agile models,
- What the Product is, and how small we can carve out *valuable* pieces of each Requirement
- How risky, or susceptible to change, are our Requirements
- How ready and stable is the software development environment and infrastructure

Most organizations end up adopting an Iteration duration of one week or two, when they achieve a relatively high degree of maturity. Very often, they start with a duration of three or four weeks; sometimes, one or two. There is no right or wrong way to determine the Sprint duration. Perhaps, the only right way is through experimentation.

There are *Pros and Cons* associated with adopting models with either shorter or longer durations. Longer durations are sometimes considered better to begin with, until 'the dust settles down'; and teams have enough experience to establish norms, before they switch to a shorter duration. On the other hand, there is a fairly good chance that teams may develop anti-patterns, which are difficult to get rid of, in the future.

At the surface, shorter durations may appear better because it allows teams to rapidly experiment, and fail fast. This helps to develop team norms much faster, aside from helping to deliver software more frequently. However, at least in the beginning, the team will go through churns more frequently; particularly, if they have to deal with ambiguous and frequently changing requirements. This also happens when the team is launched without adequate training, incomplete understanding of the process, inadequate or unstable environment and infrastructure, and so on; and, particularly, under pressure from management.

A good number of Agilists recommend the **'Shock Therapy'** – introduce and bombard teams with Agile theory and practices, in shorter iterations. Apparently, this helps teams to continuously face challenges and respond by *quickly* learning and adopting best practices. Team members are always 'on their toes', learning and performing most effectively.

I have not seen any evidence to conclude that one approach is better than the other. The general consensus is that, regardless of what approach an organization starts with, the 'ideal' duration is either one or two weeks. This is not to say that longer durations (up to one month) are not suitable at all. It all depends on each organization's culture, structure, environment, goals, objectives, and best practices.

Shorter iterations have the following advantages, enabling a better chance of success:

- Laser-sharp focus on limited scope of work,
- Fewer ambiguities and open dependencies,
- Quicker turnaround time,
- Frequent delivery,
- Rapid experimentation,
- Frequent and early feedback,
- Better ability to iterate on a requirement or feedback,
- Early detection and resolution of defects,
- Better team collaboration and motivation,
- Better dependency management,
- Lower risks,
- Tighter control on cost,
- Cost of failure is lower i.e., the cost of wastage or 'throwaway' work is limited to the maximum cost of a Sprint; amongst several others

Chapter 4: The Principle of Close Collaboration

'Business people and developers must work together daily throughout the project.'

This principle basically states that *Business and Technology people should work together every day* during the course of the project; however, it also implies that *they should be part of the same team, wherever possible*. However, in order to understand and apply this principle, we need to understand a few concepts, and dismiss few fallacies, first.

Design Thinking approaches, including the use of various tools such as the *Business Model Canvas*, or *Lean Canvas*, are required to help organizations to get a better understanding of:

- the market and its needs; as well as various aspects of the business environment
- customers and actual market demand
- product definition and product potential, amongst several others

What is the Product? It may sound paradoxical but it is quite true that several organizations struggle with various aspects of product development, on account of its **poor product definition**. The organization's structure should perhaps depend on what the product is, or how the product is defined. The team's purpose and structure depend on it. The organization of the Backlog depends on it. How teams work and collaborate depend on it. In other words, almost everything depends on how the product is defined. To address this, an analysis of the 'product problem' can start with a better assessment of the customers.

Who are our Customers? Is the product tangible like a phone, or intangible like a *Software as a Service (SaaS)* solution? Are you serving end-customers directly; or indirectly, as an intermediary? Are partners involved? Are customers internal or external?

There are **multiple product perspectives** depending on who the customer is. A large number of teams would be more focused on **their internal, limited view** of **their own product** instead of the *end-customer view of the final product*. If few teams share this view or the same perspective, a *'virtual product'* may be defined and these teams can share the same *virtual Product Backlog*. Each team may carve out its own 'portion' of this common *Product Backlog*, into its own *Team Backlog*.

Figure 3.3: Customer Profiling and Product Definition

Customers, Partners and Products

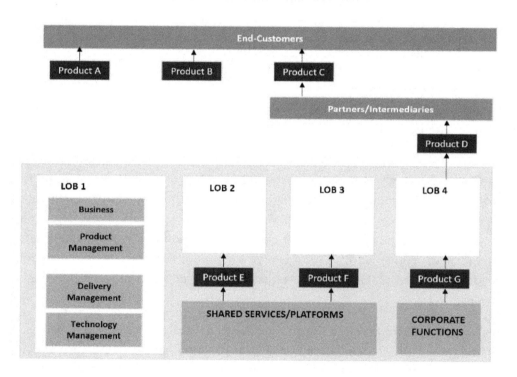

Understanding User Needs through User Journeys: Once we have adequately identified the customers, then we need to intimately understand their needs, as reflected in their **User Journeys** (journeys undertaken to accomplish their needs). This requires a careful analysis of every activity the customer undertakes. For instance, if I am hungry and need food at lunch time, I may look for a restaurant nearby or look one up online. I may drive to the restaurant or get the food delivered. I may choose between various cuisines. Once I reach the restaurant, I may have to wait to be seated, or place an order, or both. This depends on whether I want the order 'to go' and eat in. Once the order is placed and I may have paid for it, the meal is prepared in the kitchen. Once it is ready, it is served at my table. I then take the last step at fulfilling my need i.e., satisfying my hunger. Interestingly, the need may be *more specific*. Rather than satisfying my hunger with just any kind of food, I might be craving for food from a particular type of cuisine or a specific entrée. The same need may be fulfilled in an entirely different way at different times; e.g., during breakfast or dinner time. Despite these differences, the User Journey, more or less, remains the same.

There are several *constraints* as well as *permutations and combinations of these steps* or activities; and all of these have to be considered. For instance, one step may come after another in different scenarios or contexts. In few restaurants, I may have to pay at the beginning, in advance of any delivery, i.e., *Pre-pay*; as opposed to at the end, after the product or service has been delivered i.e., *Post-pay*. More often than not, each restaurant may have a limited set of products and services, depending on its specialty. For instance, an Italian restaurant may not be able to serve Kung Pao chicken. All of these constraints and scenarios must be adequately mapped out, in time, to be able to define the Product. A fairly good picture of the *Customer Profile* and *User Personas* must be developed.

Organization Structure: *Those who need to work together need to be in the same organization*. In this context, the term organization refers to a 'large department' in a large enterprise.

Successful organizations have radically and disruptively restructured their organizations to meet their needs more effectively, using an Agile model. The technology and delivery organizations are tightly aligned with the Line of Business; sometimes, within the *same* organization structure. While working at one of the world's leading data center companies, I had a unique first-hand experience. Existing organization structures were torn down to demolish walls between Business, Product Management, and Delivery teams; resulting in an organization structure as shown in Figure 3.4. This helped the organization to clearly define their products and services. It also facilitated the decomposition and structuring of the organization in a more meaningful way. However, not all organizations can afford to have radically disruptive transformations for several reasons, which are outside the scope of this book.

Figure 3.4: Agile-Focused Organization Structure

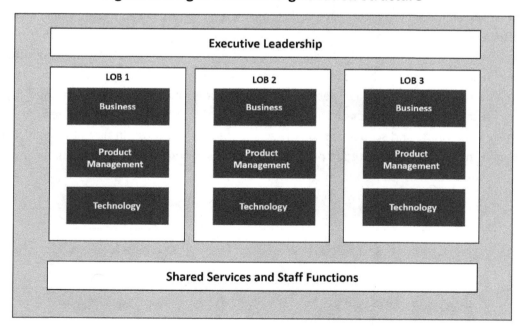

Team Structure: Once the organization's structure is designed and implemented, in alignment to customers and their User Journeys, the most critical next step may involve defining what a team, or group of teams, will do. This will determine how team, or the group of teams, will work and interact with each other.

Figure 3.5 shows a typical team structure for scrum teams organized by LOBs. It shows typical inter-team interactions, though it does not show all interactions, or interactions across Groups. Teams interact directly with each other or at a **Scrum of Scrums**. Team or Group representatives may interact at a higher level: **Scrum of Scrum of Scrums**; or something similar. Details are beyond the scope of this book. Note that each Group works on its own Product.

Figure 3.5: Team Structures and Collaboration

Backlogs: The structure of the teams, and their groupings, will determine the nature, size and variability of the Backlog. An approach I would recommend, based on my experience, is to define a *common* **Product Backlog** for a group of teams, and *individual* **Team Backlog** for each team within that group.

All requirements are initially entered in the Product Backlog. These may be in the form of Epics and Features; though each of the Epics may be continuously broken down into Stories, as much as possible. A team of **Product Managers** and **Product Owners (POs)** collaborate and *continuously* manage this Backlog. Once priorities are established, stories (not Epics or Features) are pushed *down* into Team Backlogs, based on team 'specialization' or capacity. Note that the PO of each Scrum team will be part of the team collectively managing the Product Backlog.

Figure 3.6: Product and Team Backlogs

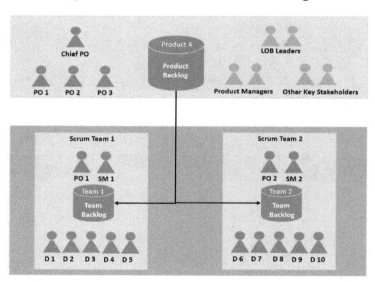

Figure 3.6 indicates one suitable way of structuring teams and Backlogs.

This approach has many advantages:

- Product Managers and LOB stakeholders, not directly associated with team, are constantly meeting Product Owners and keeping the Product Backlog up to date without disturbing Scrum teams.
- Priorities are determined through mutual consultations and agreement, on a frequent basis, rather than in isolation.
- Mutual dependencies are regularly analyzed to sequence work more effectively and reduce risks
- Each of the different teams may be given a specific type of work, if it requires specialization. For instance, if a team is focused on applying specific technical skills to achieve its goals. Shared Services teams, such as User Interface (UI) and User Experience (UX) teams, or Infrastructure teams, fall into this category. However, specialization is encouraged only if the benefits outweigh the costs. Too much specialization prevents bandwidth throttling i.e., the ability to assign work to *any* team based on their capacity. Specialized teams may be either waiting for work to come their way or backlogged severely if there is too little or too much work assigned to them, respectively.
- At the team level, there may be less time required for prioritization or planning since the POs would be actively collaborating 'all the time'
- There would be more effective coordination and collaboration, as well as risk and dependency management, such as in Scrum of Scrums.

While Scrum recommends one PO per Scrum team, organizations may decide to have more than one PO in one Scrum team, or a Chief Product as the Lead amongst several POs, similar to that proposed by the Large Scale Scrum (LeSS) model. This occurs when Product Management is a *complex* function with *multitudinous responsibilities*, or entails a *large volume of work*. Scrum recommends simplification of complex structures. Note, however, that simplified structures may lead to significant overheads in coordination and collaboration, due to increased communication channels.

Better understanding of *Customers and their needs*, as well as suitable *organization structures*, allow teams to successfully deliver solutions that delight customers. This objective can be effectively met, on a continuous basis, if the **'right' people work together at the 'right' time**.

Business stakeholders, including Product Managers, should work continuously with the *Development* or *Delivery* teams. The PO represents the *Business* and *Product Management* stakeholders, *inside* the Scrum team. It is not a part-time responsibility. The PO works with other Scrum Team members, on a wide range of activities, almost on a daily basis. Each member of the Scrum team, including the PO, is *dedicated and full-time* on the Scrum team. Scrum Team members should not be shared across teams, whenever possible. Additionally, they should not perform more than one of the three roles of the Scrum Team: Scrum Master (SM), Product Owner (PO) and Development Team.

The PO should participate in the Daily Scrum as a collaborator, and to understand what is going on a daily basis. The Daily Scrum, aka Standup, is not a status meeting; particularly, one in which the PO demands to know what the status is. It is a planning meeting for the Development Team to come together and plan for the day (the next '24 hours'). This Daily Plan will depend on how well the previous day's plan was executed, and whether the team encountered any inhibitors or blockers *aka* impediments.

The PO or the SM is NOT expected to *manage* the Daily Scrum or *manage* the Development Team. They attend the Daily Scrum to *support* the Development team, as and when needed. The SM or PO is NOT required to attend the Daily Standup; yet, many organizations get this wrong and expect the SM to schedule and facilitate the event.

The PO is advised to attend the Daily Scrum primarily for two reasons: (a) he or she can understand the progress towards the Sprint goal; and help the team tweak the plan or goal, if required. As an example, based on discussions undertaken during the Daily Scrum, the PO may assess the need to add or remove stories to the existing Sprint scope, or abnormally end the Sprint; and (b) to clarify any requirements quickly, without the need for another meeting; or identify the need to facilitate post-Standup discussions with the team, and those outside, if required.

The SM is accountable and responsible for ensuring that the Standup takes place, regularly and effectively. He may attend the Standup to facilitate the discussions, if required; particularly, when discussions become involved or animated and team loses focus, or cannot keep track of time. He is encouraged to attend so that he may be able to support the team or understand what real-time support the team needs. Helping team to resolve impediments and blockers is a key responsibility of the SM. However, it is very important to remember that team is self-organized and should be able to resolve most impediments by themselves. Only those impediments, which the Development Team may not be able to resolve by themselves, or will take away an extraordinary amount of their time from developing software, may be escalated to the SM.

Neither the SM nor PO should become a bottleneck. Development team members should not consider or make the SM or PO an admin or a postman. They should try to eliminate the 'middleman' at all times. Also, once the PO or SM gets a request for support, they should provide the necessary assistance, as much and as early as possible.

It is not advisable for team members and stakeholders to meet 'too often' since it may take precious time away from developing or delivering working software. This does not mean that we do not need to meet at all. Teams should strive to strike a balance. One way is to *limit the frequency and duration of meetings*. I recommend adding an item to the team working agreement to: (a) limit the total duration of all meetings in a day to, say, 2-3 hours; and (b) limit the total duration of all meetings in a week e.g., up to 10 hours.

Another aspect to consider is to *invite only those required* in meetings. If this is not possible, they should *mark out* in the invite clearly *who is required* and *who is not*. In any case, teams should always try to minimize the number of meetings where *all team members* are required. Note that the formal events in Scrum are required: Sprint Planning, Daily Scrum, Sprint Review and Sprint Retrospective. Backlog Refinement is another required, but informal, event.

The reason why I am elaborating on this is because the team may need to meet with various stakeholders on a regular basis. The team should work very closely with LOB and Product Management stakeholders to develop the *'right' product*. In order to develop the product in the *'right' way*, the team may need to meet frequently with 'extended' team members. These may include members of shared services, release management, infrastructure management, and other teams. Very frequently, the team may meet with other partners and interdependent teams, with or without a cadence, to discuss assumptions, resolve dependencies and address risks. If it is advisable, only few representatives of the team (not the whole team) should attend these 'non-Scrum' meetings.

Chapter 5: The Principle of Motivated Individuals

'Build projects around motivated individuals. Give them the environment and support they need, and trust them to get the job done'.

Per Scrum theory, all scrum team members are equal...there is no hierarchy. In reality, all team members are not equally knowledgeable or skilled. Also, few people are more introverted and reticent as compared to others. They may need to be motivated to speak up or assign themselves some responsibilities or tasks. For instance, in a team of 5-7 members, there will be usually be 2-3 highly motivated individuals. Rather than resort to a *carrot-or-stick* policy for optimizing performance, management should identify motivated individuals and build teams around them.

Most organizations try to always build A-teams. While this is a good strategy, it is not without pitfalls. Successful teams have a good mix of individuals with different temperaments, personalities and capabilities. The most critical factor to consider is whether the team members can gel well and perform as a cohesive unit. We should not have a team where only a few members are performing, while others are not. We also do not need a team of few heroes, who do all the work most of the time.

By means of suitable career development programs, motivated individuals should be groomed into leaders, who in turn can motivate other individuals. They can help to train and mentor *less skilled* team members. A nurturing work environment, as well as the perception that leaders are willing to listen and support teams, helps to enhance motivation. A performance-oriented recognition, reward and compensation plan is required to develop a suitable work environment.

Motivated individuals exhibit a high degree of ownership, commitment, responsibility and accountability. They are self-driven and do not wait for instructions or directions. They have an uncanny ability to determine what they need to do on a daily basis, or in the medium- or long-term. They usually have the right skills and expertise to develop high quality working software. They understand the need for frequent interactions; and communicate as well as collaborate very effectively with others. These team members can grow into servant leaders, if they already are not.

Organizations need to evaluate these characteristics of individuals in order to develop high performing, and self-managed or self-organized teams. This team, or its members, may require some occasional guidance and direction. For instance, leaders may need to articulate the organizational or product vision in a little more detail, so that team members gain a better understanding of how their work fits into the bigger scheme of things. Management and servant leaders should be able and ready to support them on a regular basis, if team members need help of any kind. Leaders and Managers, in general, should ensure that teams always have an optimal operating environment; for instance:

- development infrastructure should be highly available and reliable,
- processes do not cause unnecessary overheads
- team composition is stable; members are not being swapped in or out frequently, and so on

Chapter 6: The Principle of Face-to-Face Conversations

'The most efficient and effective method of conveying information to and within a development team is face-to-face conversation'.

All individuals within a team, or groups of teams, must work with each very frequently – perhaps, on a daily basis – and not just during the Daily Scrum. Most teams require frequent interactions during the day: during Scrum events or other activities, in order to 'move the needle'; or, make sufficient progress.

Wherever possible, teams must be **co-located**. Cost considerations, typically, drive this decision. Nevertheless, physical colocation is preferred; else, team may be virtually co-located i.e., they should be able to meet virtually, frequently, and at short notice. This generally means that team members must be located in 'friendly' time zones, which enables an overlap of working hours.

Whenever possible, teams should *not* be formed with members, who are located 'far apart', either in terms of geographical locations, or time zones. When the team is split between 'Onshore' and 'offshore', it is quite difficult to collaborate effectively. There should be an adequate overlap of working hours between the two *shores*. This applies to different locations in the same country, when there are multiple time zones. If the 'time difference' exceeds 5-8 hours, frequent collaboration is not sustainable in medium- or long-term. An appropriate way to address this is to:

- Split the team completely into independent teams, one for each location
- Optimize team structures at each location i.e., add or remove team members, as required
- Implement a 'Scrum of Scrum' between the teams, at a regular cadence, for an hour or so; only one member from each team attends regularly; as an exception, more team members attend, as required.

Teams should try to communicate and collaborate in **real time**. Email is not the ideal way to communicate, unless 'details have to be documented'. Due to its asynchronous nature, email can keep people in a 'wait mode' for an indeterminable period of time. It also reduces the 'human touch' and restricts the ability to develop a better rapport.

Body language is an important aspect of communication. *Physical meetings*, and to a certain degree, *virtual video meetings* or *phone calls* help team members to interpret non-verbal cues, signs, or signals, so that they can react appropriately. There could be a few team members who are capable of, or adept at, observing or listening to these cues. They regularly use these modes to communicate more effectively. These modes of communication also help to build better relationships. Face-to-face conversations should always be the most preferred mode of communications.

Team members should always strive to adopt a model that reduces the scope for confusion, miscommunication, and misinformation. Finally, good communication refers to the ability to get the message across; not the ability to speak a language well. Fluency in a language improves communication skills. Communication is easier when team members are conversing in their own native language. However, team members must remember that they need to converse in a common or the 'official' language, when there are participants from different backgrounds, countries or regions.

Listening skills are perhaps far more important than the ability to communicate verbally. This skill is not as common as one would think or want. Successful team members and leaders have great listening skills; and one should continuously strive to improve upon this personal trait, in order to be successful.

The suitability of one or more modes of communication may be determined by the team's, or the organization's, culture. It also depends on an individual's attitude, behavior, personality, temperament and preferences. The team should constantly attempt to strike a suitable balance between conflicting opinions or practices. Preferences and best practices may be documented in the Team's Working Agreement.

The following constitute the most effective means of communications, ranked in order of priority, but may depend on the team's specific circumstances. In general, whenever appropriate, take a top-down approach while evaluating the following options to determine the preferred mode of communications:

- Talk, face-to-face – meeting physically – one-on-one
- Talk, face-to-face – meeting virtually (video) – one-on-one
- Talk, over the phone – one-on-one
- Chat, real-time, using a chat tool – one-on-one
- Talk, face-to-face – meeting physically – few required stakeholders
- Talk, face-to-face – meeting virtually (video) – few required stakeholders
- Talk, over the phone – Conference call – few required stakeholders
- Chat, real-time, using a chat tool – few required stakeholders
- Talk, face-to-face – meeting physically – larger group of stakeholders
- Talk, face-to-face – meeting virtually (video) – larger group of stakeholders
- Talk, over the phone – Conference call – larger group of stakeholders
- Chat, real-time, using a chat tool – larger group of stakeholders
- Back-and-forth emails
- Email broadcasts

Chapter 7: The Principle of Measuring Progress

'Working software is the primary measure of progress'.

Before we dive into specifics, it is very important to note that even *experts* have fallen prey to *fallacious assumptions,* which has resulted in *inappropriate application* of *mathematical operations* to *abstract constructs* like Story Points. Unlike actual numbers, story points are notional and cannot be *typically* be subject to mathematical operations.

3 story points + 5 story points is NOT always equal to 8 points.

We are permitted to add estimates of all stories to arrive at the *Velocity* of a team. This is one time when we are allowed to apply the mathematical formula of *addition.* Similarly, we may apply the operation of *division* to compute *Predictability.*

8 points is NOT always equal to 3 story points + 5 story points.

While splitting a story, you may not be able to split an 8-point story into two stories of 3 and 5 points. It may be more meaningful to split it into 2 stories of 5 points each; if you were to account for additional efforts, risks and complexity. This is particularly true when teams have to work on these independent stories, at different times.

In short, ask yourself how often you can add 2 oranges to 2 apples. Or, would you rather consider them as 4 counts of different fruits. Let us keep this in mind whenever we consider measures or metrics, based on story points.

If there is one thing you could say Agilists are obsessed with, then, it is **working software**. The primary purpose of the team is to *produce* working software, if possible, in each iteration, in the form of a *potentially shippable* **product increment**.

The software delivered at the end of every Sprint, or Iteration, is called a **Product Increment**. It is so called because: (a) it is developed incrementally, and (b) it is built on top of an existing product or Increment. Even during new product development, an increment is produced at the end of the *first* Sprint itself.

We consider each increment to be **potentially shippable**. In other words, we should be able to *promote* each increment from the development environment to the production environment, through any staging environment, if applicable. Whenever possible, it should be shipped to customers.

The emphasis on the term 'potentially' reflects a situation in which we cannot always ship the increment to customers. This is the usually the norm in case of new product development. The team may park the *interim* software, and its increments, in a staging area until it is ready to be shipped. This staging area may be a new production environment that no one is using, until the product is completely developed and delivered. Using such an isolated production environment is recommended, wherever possible, because the environment and its configurations can be tested during each iteration.

Occasionally, there may be situations in which the team cannot deliver an increment after every iteration. Perhaps, the scope of work in that iteration may be too large and the team is not able to complete development and testing for the entire Sprint scope. Alternatively, a number of blockers and impediments may prevent the team from delivering the software, either partially or completely. Or, the team may encounter several risks, assumptions, issues, and dependencies (RAID), which inhibit the achievement of the Sprint Goal. Sometimes, the iteration is ended abnormally. Or, quite often, there are times when the focus is more on architecture and design and there's not sufficient time to develop software; particularly, if the iteration is short. Nevertheless, there are several ways to overcome each of the above adverse circumstances. Very often, the team could reduce these risks through timely 'Pre-work'.

While *Working Software* is the primary measure of progress, it is not the only measure. Organizations and teams are advised to develop suitable measures. As much as possible, the number of such measures or metrics should be limited to their use and usefulness:

- Do not specify any metric, which you cannot or will not use
- Start with only a few metrics, which can act as *Levers* to adjust performance
- Too many measures lead to ineffectiveness, resulting in confusion and chaos – akin to riding on too many boats at the same time
- To stay focused on few specific objectives or goals, use few *valid* and *reliable* measures
- As one objective get fulfilled or a desired parameter or dimension gets under control, add one or more measures to your 'metrics portfolio'.

Typically, *Velocity* and *Predictability* [13] are two important measures that organizations adopt at the beginning of their Agile implementation. Stakeholders must understand that these are nominal measures, which have value in a *relative* sense. There is no meaning in the absolute value of each measure. It does not tell the entire story. For instance:

- a velocity of 100 is *not* better than a velocity of 50
- a predictability of 100% is *not* necessarily better than a predictability of 80%

The trends are important. An upward or stable trend may be better than a downward trend. However, this may not always be so. Analysts may need to conduct a more detailed evaluation in case reports show downward trends, before concluding that the team's performance has gone down. Typically, it is an indicator of something that the team is struggling with: team members may have been swapped out, resulting in regression of the team state to 'Forming'; unstable environments resulting in the team not meeting its Sprint goal, and so on.

Note that, *prima facie*, an upward trend appears to be good. Also, note that I have not assigned any numbers or values in Figure 3.7.

Figure 3.7: Velocity and Predictability

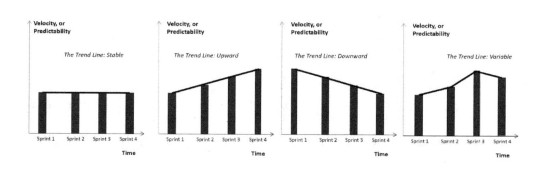

If we assume that Figure 3.7 shows the trends for four different teams, the first thing to clearly understand is that the **Velocity** measure has a connotation and interpretation, which is *very **internal** to the team*. We cannot simply compare teams based on their Velocities. One team may estimate a story at 5 points, while another team estimates it at 3 and yet another at 8. Comparing teams based on Velocity is like comparing apples with oranges.

Generally, an upward trend may be good whether it is consistent or not. Sometimes, it may not be so – it could signify a constant and conscious *under-commitment*, reflecting lack of confidence or un willingness to do more. Teams that follow the principle '*Commit Less, Deliver More*' may exhibit this characteristic.

What teams need to understand is that, increasingly, organizations are dropping the idea of Commitment as an action, as in '*Our team commits to deliver 50 story points during this Sprint*' Vs '*Our teams are committed to meeting our Sprint Goal or the Sprint Plan*', which itself could entail delivering 50 Story points. The subtle difference is that the team is *not held* to that commitment; not penalized formally; and not subjected to adverse feedback, if the team were not able to deliver 50 points. Mature organizations discourage the use of terms 'Commitments', or 'Committed' Story Points, and instead use 'Planned' Story Points.

Performance and progress can be represented in the forms of graphs and charts. The Burndown Chart, or Burnup Chart, can be used to view progress towards the Sprint or Release goal. The burndown chart shows how much work is remaining, while the burnup chart shows how much has been done. Each of these two charts gives the same information from two different perspectives. Teams may regularly use out-of-the-box charts in tools, like Jira. Burndown charts, Velocity Chart, and Sprint Reports are very commonly used. Another important one, the Version Report, allows team members to forecast when the remaining work for a specific Version/Release will be completed, if the current rate is sustained.

Metrics can be of many types, depending on what we need to measure or control. Aside from typical *delivery metrics, financial metrics* may be important. Depending on what funding models the organization adopts, these metrics could be different. For instance, an organization may keep the *funds* for a team constant, sprint after sprint. This helps to develop a **predictable budget**, sprint after sprint, quarter after quarter, year after year. This applies only if *the product is persistent*, and *teams are persistent*.

Metrics like *Average Cost per Resource* and *Average Cost Per Sprint* may help to prepare a budget, or control costs. These numbers are *easier* to compute as compared to those used in the past for *Waterfall* projects. It may *sometimes* be worthwhile to compare these metrics across teams; while it may not very appropriate at other times. Few teams may have a higher average cost due to the nature of the work they undertake, or the skills required. Specialized skills often come at a higher cost; and organizations normally have to pay a higher cost for higher quality. While organizations strive for the highest quality, it may come at a highly unreasonable cost. Quality is subject to the Theory of Marginal Utility. Beyond a certain point, the cost of achieving a marginal increase in quality may be highly disproportionate i.e., the cost may increase exponentially.

Regardless of the type and nature of the metrics, a constant evaluation must be made to determine if they provide useful information or not; or, if it adds to undue overheads. If a metric does not provide any discernable value in the medium- or long-term, it should be discontinued right away.

Chapter 8: The Principle of Sustainable Development

'Agile processes promote sustainable development. The sponsors, developers, and users should be able to maintain a constant pace indefinitely'.

Agile models are 'lightweight', with very few prescribed requirements or rules. For instance, Scrum has only a few rules to comply with so that the model can be considered Scrum; and not 'Scrum but' or 'Scrum like'. Scrum is quite simple to understand but quite difficult to master.

The simple and lightweight nature of Agile models and methodologies enable sustained development. Teams are able to implement these models fairly quickly, with a high degree of success. Stable *velocity* and *predictability* enable better forecasting, particularly, in terms of *timelines* as well as *costs*. Expectations are understood and managed better.

A high degree of stability, as opposed to variability, is preferred – in terms of outputs, outcomes and progress. A constant velocity of 50 over 3 Sprints, is considered better than an inconsistent velocity of 40, 50, and 60 over the same period of time. Note that the average velocity in either case is the same.

Sustained development is possible if the team is able to anticipate and plan its work very well over a longer period of time i.e., over two or three Sprints, at the least. If Stories are READY well before a Sprint starts, the risks are minimal. As a thumb-rule, each Scrum team must have at least 2 Sprints worth of READY stories in their Backlog. This is possible when almost all assumptions and dependencies are assessed and addressed in advance.

Execution may go into a tailspin if 'open issues', in the form of hidden requirements and open dependencies, are discovered when the team is in the middle of development or testing during a Sprint. This may result from failing to engage partners at the right time, or insufficient refinement definition or analysis. Agile processes allow for some degree of surprise, since we do not wait for the complete picture on anything to get started. However, 'gaps', if any, must be minimal; and discovery of these gaps during a Sprint should be the exception, rather than the norm. Finally, it is ok to have few 'minor' gaps in requirements, design or dependencies, if these can be quickly addressed during the

Sprint. As discussed earlier, sustained development depends on the team's ability to forecast needs, as well as address risks and dependencies, well in advance.

Leadership and Management, including the Sponsors and Promoters, should be able to provide all necessary support for the team. This could imply proper budgets, directions, and vision. Or, tactical issues such as expedited resolution of impediments and escalated requests. There should be a regular forum where team members may bring their support requests; or, tools which help to channelize these requests to the right Leaders, in a timely manner.

Leaders should not have unrealistic expectations or demands. They should have great observation and listening skills to better understand what teams really need or want. Medium- and long-term success is based on consistency and sustainability; and not sporadic spectacular achievements. Teams do not really need heroes. They need members with the ability to consistently work well together, in order to meet goals in a sustainable way. Leaders and team members need to give more attention to **qualitative** aspects of software development, such as *motivation* and *morale*, rather than just the *quantitative*.

Figure 3.8: Sprint Events and Activities

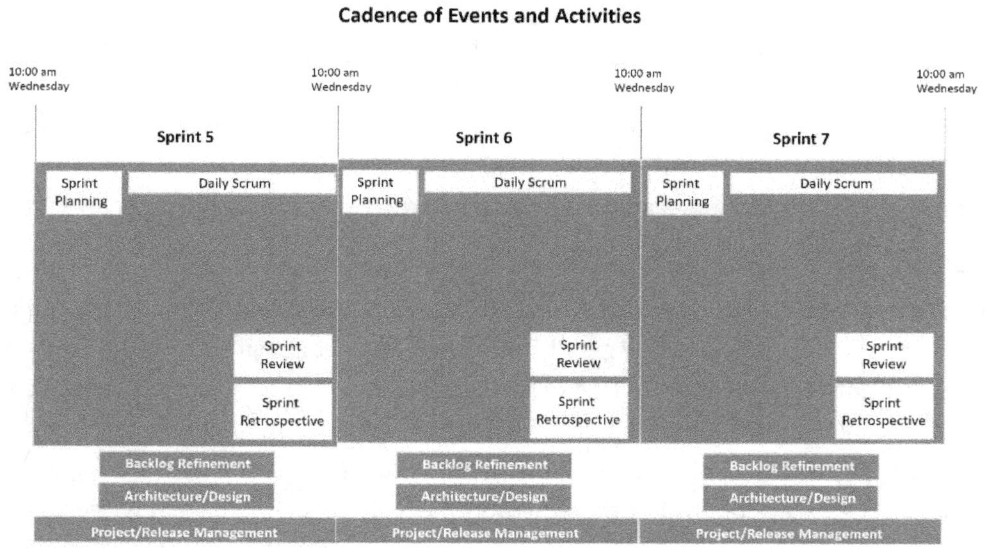

Cadence of Events and Activities

One of the fallacies, which arises from an incorrect or incomplete understanding of Agile methodologies, or Scrum terminology, is that *'everything occurs in the Sprint'*. In a way, it would be correct if this statement were to be modified slightly: Everything *does* occur during the Sprint *timeline*; but, not necessarily *in* the Sprint.

Only the work towards fulfilling a Sprint goal, i.e., the Sprint Scope reflected in the Sprint Backlog, *occurs within the Sprint*. The **four formal Scrum events** occur within the Sprint. The fifth informal event i.e., **Backlog refinement** and other *required* activities occur during the same timelines but not in the Sprint.

'Pre-work' i.e., work completed before Sprint starts, enables sustainable development. These required activities could entail involvement of team members on project and release activities, which other teams are also involved with.

Few team members may be involved in *risk, assumption, issue, and dependency (RAID) management*. The entire team, or a select few, may be involved in **Refinement** aka *Backlog Refinement* or *Grooming*[14]. The following considerations should be assessed while assigning team members to each of these activities. This will help to maximize the time spent of software development, as well as reduce risks:

- 'Pre-work' should be done a few Sprints in advance. This applies to Refinement activities and well as RAID management. This will ensure that a sufficient number of stories are READY for intake into a Sprint, with the minimum risk.
- Strike a balance *on time and resources* allocated between *Pre-work* Vs *Sprint scope*. For instance, a maximum of 20% of the team's time may be spent on Pre-work **for subsequent Sprints**; and, not all team members be involved in these activities. For instance, in a seven-member team, two can represent the team and may be tasked to develop the architecture or design; perhaps, working with other teams, architects, and designers.
- A *regular cadence for Refinement* is highly encouraged; but the timing and duration should be optimal. Sometimes, it may be prudent to spend one entire day to this activity. This helps to generate more focus and avoid context switching, such as between the refinement activities and 'real work'. However, team members may not be equally attentive, productive and effective all throughout a day-long session. Other teams prefer to do this in 'chunks' at

---

[14] Officially, this activity is referred to as 'Refinement'. Teams may use 'Backlog Refinement' often to clarify the purpose; but, use of the very old term 'grooming' must be discontinued or discouraged.

different times during a week. For instance, teams assign 3-4 hours a week per a regular cadence.

- Set up a cadence for each activity you do regularly; aside from the cadence for the formal events. And, please do remember: Use a meeting or event only if you need it. Cancel or reschedule if you do not need a meeting, which has already been set up per a cadence. Do **NOT** meet just because the meeting is on the calendar. The only exceptions to this rule are **ALL** formal Scrum Events, and *not just* the Daily Scrum.

A Sprint always starts when a previous one ends. There are no gaps between Sprints, even if the team is not working at that time. For instance, if a team's Sprint ends at midnight, the next Sprint starts at one second past midnight. Most teams, probably, are not working at that time; but you may be surprised to know that some do. Nonetheless, for a regular team, the *Sprint Start* and *End* timings should be suitably determined and held constant. While teams may start a Sprint on Monday at 9:00 am, it may be preferable to start on Tuesday or Wednesday at 10:00 am. This allows team members to settle in and prepare for the day, before the *Daily Scrum* starts. Developers tend to work late and their creative juices seem to flow better later in the day; when they develop a better focus and momentum, free from distractions. Scheduling a *Daily Scrum* too early may consistently result in either few team members showing up late, or not showing up at all. The purpose of the Standup is not fulfilled if this occurs regularly.

'Happy Fridays' tend to be 'light' working days. Team members tend to 'switch off' early, in readiness for the weekend, even if they stay till the end of the working day. Few team members may leave early on Fridays, say 2-3 pm. A long commute home could be one reason why; and there could be several others. Similarly, team members recovering from *'Monday Morning Blues'* may not perform efficiently during the first few hours on Mondays, if not over the entire day.

The above factors need to be taken into account while determining the Sprint duration, the Start and End times, as well as 'productive' hours during the day – typically, 6 hours in an 8-hour work day. These factors also impact several other aspects of the Sprint – the timing, duration, and effectiveness of the Sprint Events, the viability of a Sprint Backlog, and so on. Teams should never be forced, explicitly or implicitly, to work extra hours to meet 'stringent' deadlines. Leaders should never create *artificial* emergencies or contingencies.

Chapter 9: The Principle of Technical Excellence

'Continuous attention to technical excellence and good design enhances agility'.

Teams may be familiar with the concept of _emergent_, or _evolving_ architecture and design. Some believe the _architecture is emerging_, while the _design is evolving_. Others totally disagree and insist that, to a large extent, an upfront architecture is required before any evolution can take place during Sprints. Regardless of how much architecture is done upfront, both the architecture and design will evolve with time. This may happen at a fast pace, or a slower pace, depending on the _need_ as well as _competence_ of the teams involved. In other words, we need the skilled team members to be involved in this effort. The better their skills, the better will be the architecture and design; and their long-term usefulness.

Technical excellence and good architecture, or design, interact as if in a closed loop system. A good architecture is realized if the team creating this comprises high skilled experts. A quick review of the architecture may highlight improvement areas, which the team can quickly address. This may lead to discovery of new problems and solutions. The team may acquire new knowledge or skills, which they then apply to enhance the design. It would be an understatement to mention that technical excellence is required across all facets of development: front-end, middle-tier, or back-end development; database design and administration; system and network administration; pipeline, environment and infrastructure management; and so on.

There is an increasing need for technical excellence, in an increasingly complex world of software development. This new wave is characterized by rapid adoption of the XaaS or Cloud paradigm, CI/CD, microservices architecture, APIs, artificial intelligence, robotics, and to a certain degree, _Serverless computing_ or _Functions as a Service_. Developing requirements, architecture, design and the code itself, in an _incremental manner_ increases the chances of success. Nonetheless, the team should continually look at the big picture; and constantly review how the pieces fit or interact together as a whole.

Technical excellence is achieved through continuous learning and regular collaboration. This enhances interactive exchanges and application of knowledge and skills. In order to achieve Technical Excellence, there are few concepts that team members need to be have deep expertise in:

- DevOps and DevSecOps
- Continuous Integration/ Continuous Delivery/Continuous Deployment (CI/CD)
- Test-Driven Development (TDD/ATDD/BDD)
- Architectural Runway, Emergent Design, and Silent Design
- Design Thinking
- SOLID Principles
- XaaS (X as a Service, where X is one of the following: Infrastructure, Platform, Software, Application, Database, and so on)
- The Twelve Factor App
- Cloud Native Applications and Microservices Architecture
- Site/Software Reliability Engineering (SRE)

DevOps/DevSecOps

Very often, teams consider *DevOps* to be the same thing as *CI/CD*. Nothing could be further from the truth. The DevOps model is an outcome of learnings from various Agile methodologies, which appeared more relevant than traditional methodologies like *ITIL* (formerly *Information Technology Infrastructure Library*). A significant principle that underlines the concept of *DevOps* is that *Development* and *Operations* teams collaborate and work together, more or less, as parts of the same team. In addition, this model encompasses Shared-Services teams, such as the Infrastructure and Platform teams. The processes and practices of all these teams are integrated seamlessly to cover every aspect of the development and delivery process: coding, configuration, testing, building, packaging, deployment, release, alerting, monitoring, failover, self-healing, resilience, reliability, and so on.

In the past, these two teams usually operated in silos. The Development team considered their responsibilities complete once they promoted their code to Production. They expected the Operations team to 'completely take over' any future maintenance of the code. Very often, this resulted in inadequate 'support levels', quality issues, and poor customer experience. The primary reasons were twofold: (a) Operations team members do not have deep knowledge about the code and its functionality, at least as well as Development team members do; and (b) a 'small' Ops team, with only a few members typically, is expected to support a large portfolio of applications. This resulted in team members being 'spread too thin' across many applications in their portfolio; thereby preventing them from putting in a worthwhile effort on each application.

With explosive growth in virtualization in the last few years, the need for managing physical infrastructure has become lower. However, this 'infrastructure environment' has become increasingly complex with a mix of *bare-metal* and *virtualized* server environments. Teams are increasingly relying on *virtual machines* and *containers*, which in turn require sophisticated cluster or container management systems, like Kubernetes. In recent years, *Cloud Service Providers* have been championing the use of *Network Function Virtualization (NFV)* and *Software Defined Networks (SDN)*. Routers, Switches, Load Balancers, Firewalls, VPNs, SD-WAN are now available as *virtualized Value-added services*. Open-Source software has become highly popular, as organizations shy away from huge investments or recurring license costs. In the new DevOps world, all these services are expected to be available on demand.

The DevOps model became very popular after the publication of the book '*The DevOps Handbook*', authored by Gene Kim, Patrick Debois, Jez Humble and John Willis. This book is a 'must read'[15].

With the incorporation of *Security* into this model, per a 'shift-left' paradigm, the DevSecOps model requires Security to be a consideration from the very beginning of the Discovery and Development process. A very good understanding of standards and best practices, such as *Open Web Application Security Project® (OWASP) Top 10*, is essential to make software secure in a highly vulnerable digital world.

---

[15] The DevOps Handbook: How to Create World-Class Agility, Reliability, and Security in Technology Organizations (2016)

Continuous Integration/Continuous Delivery/Continuous Deployment (CI/CD)

The concepts and practices of **CI/CD** lie at the heart of the **DevOps** model, and this is the reason why most people consider these two concepts to be one and the same. It must be noted that CI/CD is based on one *critical aspect of DevOps: the 'toolchain'*. The toolchain comprises various toolsets of the *entire* team, integrated in a seamless fashion. A large segment of this toolchain is what we refer to as the 'CI/CD pipeline', using Jenkins (and previously, Hudson, before it became obsolete).

Since teams are very familiar with these practices, I will not delve into any details, except than to highlight the following:

- **Continuous Integration**: Continuous integration with the main line: Developers pull from the Repo before coding; integrate code with shared Repo multiple times in a day; and resolve merge conflicts. Each check-in triggers automated tests and builds.
- **Continuous Delivery**: Continuously deployed automatically to a non-Production environment; potentially deployable, but not deployed to Production
- **Continuous Deployment**: Continuously deployed *to Production* (Customers) in an automated fashion, with no human intervention.

Test-Driven Development (TDD)

Again, a topic very familiar to Development teams. This Development approach, based on the 'test first' concept of Extreme Programming (XP), and focuses on:

- First creating a test harness, and writing only a bit of code, which makes a test pass; next, write code only for the next test that failed, and so on; refactor, as required
- Converting the requirements into test cases first

Acceptance Test-Driven Development (ATDD)

While ATDD is also a *development-focused approach* of writing tests, it is not truly a developer 'tool' for writing code using a specific way, as prescribed by TDD. It is focused on *Acceptance Testing* by business stakeholders, or those representing them. This approach highlights all the scenarios that business stakeholders consider essential to determine that the requirements have been met. It approach enables tests to be written in a clear and concise manner. This helps Developer and Testers to get a clear or better understanding of the requirements. Those familiar with the User Story approach will realize that the development and testing is driven by the Acceptance Criteria.

Behavior Driven Development (BDD)

BDD is closely related to TDD, and extends the concept to reflect User Behavior. It requires unit testing, and thereby unit code, to correspond to actual user behavior. Tests are written in snippets, which reflect a specific usage scenario, typically using a simple Domain-specific Language (DSL) like *Gherkin*, when *Cucumber* is the tool used for implementing BDD. More details are beyond the scope of this book.

Architectural Runway and Emergent Design

Practitioners of the **Scaled Agile Framework (SAFe)** will be familiar with this term. The *Architectural Runway* 'consists of the *existing code*, *components*, and *technical infrastructure* needed to implement *near-term features* without excessive redesign and delay'[16]. It is considered a foundation on which new features or capabilities are implemented; and is based on **Emergent Design**, 'the process of discovering and extending the architecture only as necessary to implement and validate the next increment of functionality'[17]. The SAFe Agile architecture strategy 'supports Agile development practices through collaboration, emergent design, intentional architecture, and design simplicity' [18] Globally, it is widely accepted that some degree of **intentional architecture** should be continuously undertaken, without any Big Design Up-front. Another thing to be noted is that Apple is a big proponent of the **'Intentional Design'** concept.

The reader is encouraged to explore the topics highlighted in this section, some of which are beyond the scope of this book.

---

[16] Architectural Runway, © Scaled Agile, Inc.
[17] Emergent Design, © Scaled Agile, Inc.
[18] Agile Architecture, © Scaled Agile, Inc.

Chapter 10: The Principle of Maximizing Simplicity

'Simplicity–the art of maximizing the amount of work not done–is essential'.

Some of us are perfectionists. We never 'give up' until we think our work product is 'perfect'. We keep 'fine-tuning' our requirements, design, and code until it is perceived to be 'excellent' and something to be very proud of. While this in itself is not bad, it may come at a high cost. A number of dependent stakeholders may be waiting on our work product; or, even worse, we may be neglecting other high priority work, while we chase perfection on one. Very often, we may be spending too much time on the bells and whistles, which the customer does not need or care too much about. It has been reported that over 50% of the software that the industry develops is neither used nor ever required. These extraneous features were based on faulty assumptions, or someone's attempt at self-actualization. Elegant software does not have to be complex. There is elegance in simplicity. 'Straight-forward' or simple design or code may be easier to understand and maintain. Complex code may have performance overheads, aside from creating nightmares for support and maintenance staff. A balance may be required between *too simple* and *too complex* design or code.

Apple, and its products, are renowned for **user experience** through their *simplistic* and *minimalist*, yet *aesthetic* designs and user interfaces. The only two things that determine the usefulness of any software are: (a) overall usability, and (b) features, which clients *actually* need. Often, clients *may* not be able to tell what they need. The ability to discern between *invalid assumptions* and *proactive determination of client needs* is a key factor of success. It distinguishes innovative, *current* market leaders like Apple and Samsung, from the *prior* market leaders like Blackberry, Nokia and Sony. The latter group of organizations are reinventing themselves or rediscovering their USPs to be more up-to-date with current market needs.

Processes and structures must be simple. Those familiar with the *Rational Unified Process (RUP)* will be able to relate to this. RUP, as it was conceived, was an excellent model. It had several variations to meet different needs of different organizations: software to be developed; team and organization sizes; and so on. Different 'sub-models' of RUP were based on the complexity of these needs: simple, medium, and high. However, it was perceived to be a very complex framework or model. As a result, many organizations shied away from even considering RUP as a basis for their SDLC models. Nonetheless, there were several organizations, which championed and implemented RUP, in some degree or form. In my own experience, we were able to successfully implement *parts* of RUP after we adapted the model to our needs. In a similar manner, quite a few organizations have responded to the **Scaled Agile Framework (SAFe)** in a lukewarm manner. SAFe, which may have been built on a basis or foundation similar to RUP, also prescribes *various options* for various types and size of organizations and their teams. For organizations with Scaling needs, SAFe is considered a good model to adopt. Or not. A fairly large number of organizations have not adopted SAFe; and there may be two reasons for this:

- The Framework is too complicated or complex
- Organizations have chosen to cherry pick parts of different models to develop their own

The primary reason why Scrum is so popular is that it is very simple to understand and practice...at least, to a large degree.

To summarize, it is equally important, *if not more*, for the team to decide *what **NOT** to do* as compared to *what to do*. Teams should minimize ***muda*[19]** or waste. This applies to:

- anything that is not required or desired
- requirements, design, code or any work product
- anything that leads to process overheads
- anything that does not contribute to working software
- *irrelevant* personal or individual preferences
- anything that does not have a positive impact or benefit, and so on

Finally, note that we should value *team* decisions more than *individual* opinions; and, teams should collectively make decisions, whenever possible and practical. Consensus is desired; otherwise, democratic decisions are good. Always, chase simplicity over complexity.

---

[19] Japanese term, meaning *useless* or *waste*, as used in Lean models like Toyota Production System (TPS)

Chapter 11: The Principle of Self-Organizing Teams

'The best architectures, requirements, and designs emerge from self-organizing teams'.

What exactly is a Self-organized team?

A self-organized team[20] refers to the team's ability to **_get together voluntary_**, without direction, to _perform their activities;_ and collectively _decide HOW work gets done_ to _deliver working software and other artifacts._

Important corollaries:

- Teams do not necessarily 'self-manage', i.e., one team member does not manage another
- Managers are not always required to guide their day-to-day activities
- Nobody outside the team needs to tell the team _when_ and _how_ to perform their duties; particularly, once a Sprint goal is established
- Team members quickly identify what they need to do, and focus on getting it done as quickly and independently, as much as possible; when needed, they will seek help and collaboration to complete the work, as quickly as possible
- Teams discuss WHAT needs to be done; distributes work amongst themselves and goes off individually to do their own work
- Team members come back together, or on a one-on-one basis, if they need to discuss anything or need each other's help; They do a similar thing when they need to work with other teams
- Team Members do NOT wait...they act urgently, appropriately, and avoid delays
- Teams do not depend on anyone outside the team, as much as possible
- Team members work on resolving dependencies or impediments, on their own, as much as possible. They escalate to the Scrum Master, Management and Leaders when impediments, risks and issues are beyond their control

---

[20] The Scrum Guide now refers to this team characteristic as 'self-managed'

To summarize, Self-organized teams must have individuals who exhibit high degree of ownership, dedication, commitment, responsibility and accountability.

According to Bruce Tuckman, teams go through various stages of group development: Forming, Storming, Norming, and Performing. Later, he added one more stage – Adjourning – when the team is disbanded. This popular Tuckman Model, later extended by Tom Edison, is shown in Figure 3.9. The functional 'half' on the left as displayed below was specified by Tuckman, and the dysfunctional 'half' by Edison. This model indicates that high performing team tend to become complacent and performance starts to 'decay' and dysfunction starts to set in. Proponents of the popular 'Edge of Chaos' [21] theory recommend intentionally injecting some degree of instability into the team to shake off the lethargy and promote creativity. This would set off the team to transform and achieve a higher level of performance.

Figure 3.9: Tuckman-Edison Model

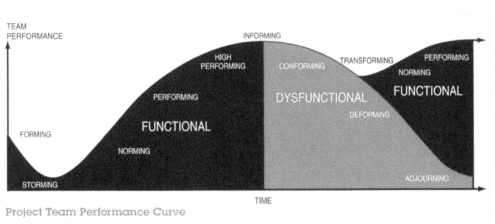

Source: Edison T. The Team Development Life Cycle: A New Look. In: Defense AT&L.

---

[21] Physicist Norman Packard propounded the Chaos theory and coined the term Edge of Chaos; and proposed that self-organization and order emerges at the edge of chaos. Other thinkers built upon this theory. This includes Dr. Robert Bilder, who observed that 'truly creative changes and the big shifts occur right at the edge of chaos'.

Teams become self-organized when they gain a higher degree of 'Agile Maturity'. This generally occurs during the Performing Stage. When teams become self-organized, they become High Performing.

Skilled self-organized teams are very successful in achieving their short-term and long-term goals. They are able to determine how much time to assign to each activity and what degree of focus is required. If they feel that their efforts are blocked for any reason, they are able to resolve these themselves or get these resolved. In some cases, they may swiftly change track, or move on to the task or story, with next highest priority.

They tend to acquire skills very rapidly. Strong communication and collaborations help them to perform very well as a team. As a result of their efforts, they are able to constantly hone their skills to develop better requirements, architecture, design, code, and test suites. This is an ongoing process and never ends, as long as the team is together. If the team disbands, or team members get reassigned, it become quite difficult to become highly self-organized again. It will take a fair amount of time to 'regain lost ground'.

Finally, it may be noted that the term 'self-organized' is not generally used in the context of *individuals*. However, *self-discipline*, in association with the individual's *other* traits described earlier, help the individual as well as the team succeed on various fronts.

Chapter 12: The Principle of Retrospection – Reflect and Adjust

'At regular intervals, the team reflects on how to become more effective, then tunes and adjusts its behavior accordingly'.

Agile practitioners are very familiar with the _three pillars of Scrum_: **Transparency, Inspection and Adaptation**; or the phrase: **Inspect and Adapt**. Team members should, every now and then, take some time to 'reflect and adjust' on any critical action they take. This is relevant to every kind of activity that the team undertakes: capturing and analyzing requirements; development and testing, for instance.

The concept of _'Inspect and Adapt'_ is based on the twin notions of **Introspection** and **Retrospection**. Every _individual_ should be constantly striving to improve every aspect of life, wherever and whenever possible, via introspection and retrospection. This applies to our work life as well as our work. In a similar way, the principle of **Retrospection** can be applied by an _individual_, a _team_ or a _group of teams_ at various departmental or organizational levels.

If we take a certain decision after evaluating various alternatives, and act upon it, we must assess whether it produced the desired or expected results. If the decision did not yield desired results, we adapt to deal with the current circumstances; and use any incremental learning we gained to make a 'better' decision the next time. Scrum is considered an empirical model because we constantly use incremental data or information that we gain along the way. Insights from observations and experience should guide us to appropriately adapt our behavior in future.

A significant number of practitioners believe that the _Sprint Retrospective_ provides the only opportunity to _Inspect and Adapt_. This is not true. Retrospection is supposed to be a continuous activity, either at an individual or team level. However, we do set time aside to conduct a retrospective formally, at a team level, at the end of every Sprint. Both introspection and retrospection are essential characteristics recommended per Agile principles.

Each of the Scrum events provides an opportunity to _formally_ inspect and adapt a specific element or area, as specified in Table 3.2.

Table 3.2: Inspect and Adapt

Event	Primary Purpose	Inspect and Adapt
Sprint Planning	Develop and Review Sprint Plan	The primary objective for this event is to *create a Sprint Plan*. However, it may entail reviewing a tentative plan created ahead of time and adjust it based on current circumstances, such as current team capacity, readiness of stories, business objectives, Product Goal, Sprint Goal, and high-priority/time-sensitive requirements, and so on. It provides an opportunity to review a longer-term *Release Plan*, if available.
Daily Scrum	Review Sprint Goal, and Develop Daily Plan	The primary objective for this event is inspect progress towards the Sprint Goal, and *create the **current day's Plan***. However, it may entail reviewing the outcome (accomplishment, blockers and gaps) of the previous day's plan, and adjust the current day's Plan accordingly. It also provides an opportunity to review the Sprint Plan, with any alternative way to achieve the Sprint Goal, if applicable.
Sprint Review	Review the Product and Sprint Outcomes	The primary objective for this event is to *review the **Product Increment** with key stakeholders and gather their feedback to enhance the Product*. This feedback is expected to enhance alignment with business goals, customer needs and experience. The team must evaluate this feedback and adapt the Product Increment accordingly. In other words, we embrace the changes recommended by key stakeholders and incorporate the *required* changes in the next *appropriate* opportunity via prioritization. The team also reviews the Sprint's outcome and discusses next steps.
Sprint Retrospective	Review the Team, Tools and Processes	The primary objective for this event is to *review the individuals, interactions, processes, tools, and their Definition of Done (**Process as well as team dynamics and working environment**) if required, create an improvement plan*. Are there any process improvements required? Did any environmental issues impact the Sprint? Is there any opportunity to improve team dynamics or team member behavior? If so, how to best address issues and opportunities for improvement, going forward?
Refinement	Review the Backlog vis-à-vis the Product Goal	The primary objective for this event is to *review the **Backlog vis-à-vis the Product Goal***, so that we can continually refine the Epics, Features and Stories and adapt per changing needs and priorities. The overall goal is to have sufficient stories ready for intake into a Sprint. Typically, there should be READY stories in advance, enough for 2 Sprints.

Index

www.ingramcontent.com/pod-product-compliance
Lightning Source LLC
LaVergne TN
LVHW081347050326
832903LV00024B/1359